MICHAELMAS AND
THE SOUL-FORCES OF MAN
(formerly: ANTHROPOSOPHY AND
THE HUMAN GEMÜT)

By
RUDOLF STEINER

ANTHROPOSOPHIC PRESS
SPRING VALLEY   NEW YORK

The four lectures in this volume were given in Vienna, September 27 to October 1, 1923. In the Collected Edition of Rudolf Steiner's works, the volume containing the German texts is entitled, *Der Jahreskreislauf als Atmungsvorgang der Erde und die vier grossen Festeszeiten* (Vol. 223 in the Bibliographic Survey). They were translated by Samuel and Loni Lockwood.

COVER DESIGN
MOTIF: GERARD WAGNER
LETTERING: PETER STEBBING

Printed in the United States of America

Contents

INTRODUCTION

Michaelmas and the Soul-Forces of Man

Reflections on the Michael Thought in its True Aspect — the Regeneration of the Michael Festival.

At Michaelmas, 1923 for the last time in his earthly life Rudolf Steiner was able to celebrate fully a Michaelmas festival, and this he did in Vienna, the capital city of his own homeland, where he had spent so many fruitful years in his youth. Much of Germany, including Berlin, was cut off from him in that year of uncontrolled inflation, but here in Vienna he could feel himself truly at home, as he refounded the Anthroposophical Society in Austria and gave these wonderful lectures on the human Gemüt.

In his Christmas letter to the members that forms part of the Michael Mystery Rudolf Steiner in 1924 emphasized in a single marvelously compressed paragraph the task of man especially in the middle period of the age of the consciousness soul in which we are now living:

"In its essential nature the Spiritual Soul (Consciousness Soul) is not cold. It seems to be so only at the commencement of its unfolding, because at that stage it can only reveal the light-element in its nature, and not as yet the cosmic warmth in which it has indeed its origin."

This cosmic warmth must now be breathed out by men into their observing of the external world. Not only must we *understand* the world objectively after the manner of the scientist, but we must enter into this understanding with our life of *feeling*, and thus wrest the world from Ahriman's clutches, filling it with the Christ forces working from within ourselves. In this short cycle, as also in the two public lectures *(Supersensible Knowledge as a Demand of the Age*, and *Anthroposophy and the Ethical-Religious Conduct of Life)* Steiner describes just how it is possible to enter into the external world with love, endowing it with soul-warmth, in the process learning also to celebrate a new kind of autumn festival in which Michael can truly participate. As soon as he returned to Dornach from Vienna, Steiner gave the five Archangel lectures *(The Four Seasons and the Archangels)*, to which these four are a soul-warming introduction that he could perhaps never have given elsewhere than in the *gemütlich* city of Vienna.

Stewart C. Easton

PUBLISHER'S NOTE

Rudolf Steiner presented the lectures printed in this volume to an audience familiar with Anthroposophy. The reader who wishes fully to appreciate this volume and who has no prior acquaintance with Anthroposophy can gain the requisite background by reading AN OUTLINE OF OCCULT SCIENCE or THEOSOPHY. These are Steiner's own introductions. Both books are published by the Anthroposophic Press.

Translator's Note

When a wholly untranslatable word occurs in a text there is no adequate alternative to retaining it. The dictionary translates *Gemüt* as "heart, soul, mind", seeming to imply, "take your choice". But the word *Gemüt* must not be thought of as having these three separate meanings, but rather as a unified concept embracing all three. Let us think of *Gemüt,* then, as meaning something like

> *the mind warmed by a loving heart and*
> *stimulated by the soul's imaginative power.*

Or again, it might be described as

> *the soul in a state of unconscious intuition*
> *arising from the working together of heart and mind.*

It is a very beautiful and comprehensive word with which every student of anthroposophy should be on intimate terms—a statement amply confirmed by a sentence that occurs in the text:

> "This human Gemüt dwells in the very
> center of the soul life." (Steiner.)

I

WHEN anthroposophy is discussed in certain circles today, one of the many misstatements made about it is that it is intellectualistic, that it appeals too predominantly to the scientific mind, and that it does not sufficiently consider the needs of the human *Gemüt*. For this reason I have chosen *Anthroposophy and the Human Gemüt* as the subject of this short cycle of lectures which, to my great satisfaction, I am able to deliver to you here in Vienna, my dear friends.

The human *Gemüt* has indeed been wholly excluded from the domain of cognition by the intellectualistic development of civilization in the last three or four centuries. It is true that today one never tires of insisting that man cannot stop short at what the dry, matter-of-fact intellect can comprehend. Nevertheless, when it is a case of acquiring knowledge people depend exclusively upon this intellect. On the other hand, it is constantly being emphasized that the human *Gemüt* ought to come into its own again—yet it is not given the chance to do so. It is denied the opportunity of making any contact whatever with cosmic enigmas, and its sphere of action is limited to the most intimate concerns of men, to matters that are decided only in the most personal way.

Today we shall discuss first in what I might call a sort of historical retrospect how, in earlier periods of human evolution, this *Gemüt* was granted a voice in the search for knowledge, when it was permitted to conjure up grandiose and mighty images before the human soul, intended to illuminate man's efforts of realizing

1

his incorporation into the body of world events, into the cosmos, and his participation in the changing times. In those days when the human *Gemüt* was still allowed to contribute its share in the matter of world views, these images really constituted the most important element of them. They represented the vast, comprehensive cosmic connections and assigned man his position in them.

In order to create a basis for further study of the human *Gemüt* from the viewpoint of anthroposophy, I should like to present to you today one of those grandiose, majestic images that formerly were intended to function as I have indicated. It is at the same time one of those images especially fitted, at present, to be brought before men's souls in a new manner, with which we shall also deal. I should like to talk to you about that image with which you are all familiar, but whose significance for human consciousness has gradually partly faded, partly suffered through misconception: I refer to the image of *the conflict, the battle, of Michael with the Dragon*. Many people are still deeply affected by it, but its more profound content is either dim or misunderstood. At best it makes no such close contact with the human *Gemüt* as was once the case, even as late as the 18th Century. People of today have no conception of the changes that have taken place in this respect, of how great a proportion of what so-called clever people call fantastic visions constituted the most serious elements of the ancient world views. This has been preëminently the case with the image of Michael's combat with the Dragon.

Nowadays, when a man reflects upon his development on the earth, a materialistic world view inclines him to trace his relatively more perfect human form back to less perfect ones, farther and farther back to physical-animal forbears. In this way one really moves away from present-day man who is able to experience his own being in an inner, psycho-spiritual way, and arrives at far more material creatures from whom man is supposed

2

to have descended—creatures that stood much closer to material existence. People assume that matter has gradually developed upward to the point where it experiences spirit. That was not the view in comparatively recent times: it was really the exact opposite.

Even as late as the 18th Century, when those who had not been infected by the materialistic viewpoint and frame of mind—there were not yet many who were so infected—cast their inner gaze back to prehistoric mankind, they looked upon their ancestors not as beings less human than themselves but as beings more spiritual. They beheld beings in whom spirituality was so inherent that they did not assume physical bodies in the sense that people on earth do today. Incidentally, the earth did not even exist then. They beheld beings living in a higher, more spiritual way and having—to express it crudely—a body of much finer, more spiritual substance. To that sphere one did not assign beings like present-day men but more exalted ones—beings having at most an etheric body, not a physical one.—Such, approximately, were our ancestors as people then conceived them.

People used to look back at a time when there were no so-called higher animals either, when at most there were animals whose descendants of the jelly-fish kind live in the oceans of today. On what was the ancestor of our earth, they represented, so to speak, the animal kingdom, the plane below that of man; and above the latter was the kingdom embracing only beings with at most an etheric body. What I enumerated in my *Occult Science, an Outline,* as beings of the higher hierarchies would still be today, though in a different form, what was then considered in a certain sense the ancestry of man.

These beings—Angeloi, Archangeloi, and Archai—in the stage of their evolution of that time, were not destined to be free beings in the sense in which today we speak of freedom in connection with man. The will of these beings was not experienced by them in such a way as to give them that singular feeling we

3

express by the phrase: to desire something arbitrarily. These beings desired nothing arbitrarily; they willed what flowed into their being as divine will; they had completely identified their will with the divine will. The divine beings ranking above them and signifying, in their interrelationships, the divine guidance of the world—these beings willed, in a sense, through the lower spirits—archangels and angels; so that the latter willed absolutely according to the purpose and in the sense of superior, divine-spiritual will.

The world of ideas of this older mankind was as follows: In that ancient epoch the time had not yet arrived in which beings could develop who would be conscious of the feeling of freedom. The divine-spiritual world-order had postponed that moment to a later epoch, when a number of those spirits, identified with the divine will, were, in a sense, to receive a free will of their own. That was to occur when the right time had come in world evolution.—It is not my purpose to corroborate today from the anthroposophical viewpoint what I have been characterizing; that will be done in the next lectures. Today I am merely describing the conceptions occupying the most enlightened spirits even as late as the 18th Century. I shall present them historically, for only by this method shall we arrive at a new view of the problem of reviving these conceptions in a different form.

But then—as these people saw it—among these spirits, whose real cosmic destiny was to remain identified with the will of the divine spirits, there arose a number of beings that wanted to disassociate their will, as it were, to emancipate it, from the divine will. In superhuman pride, certain beings revolted because they desired freedom of will before the time had come for their freedom to mature; and the most important one of these beings, their leader, was conceived of as the being taking shape in the *Dragon* that *Michael combats*—Michael, who remained above in the realm of those spirits that wanted to continue molding their will to the divine-spiritual will above them.

4

By thus remaining steadfast within the divine-spiritual will, Michael received the impulse to deal adequately with the spirit that grasped at freedom prematurely, if I may put it that way; for the forms possessed by the beings of the hierarchy of the Angeloi, Archangeloi, and Archai were simply not adapted to a being destined to have a free will, emancipated from divine will, as described. Not until later in world evolution were such forms to come into being, namely, the human form.—But all this is conceived as happening in a period in which cosmic development of the human form was not yet possible; nor were the higher animal forms possible—only the low ones I mentioned.

Thus a form had to come into being that might be called cosmically contradictory, and the refractory spirit had to be poured into this mold, so to speak. It could not be an animal form like those destined to appear only later, nor could it be the form of an animal of that time, of the then prevalent softer matter, so to say. It could only be an animal form differing from any that would be possible in the physical world, yet resembling an animal by reason of representing a cosmic contradiction. And the only form that could be evolved out of what was possible at that time is the form of the Dragon. Naturally it was interpreted in various ways when painted or otherwise represented—more or less suitably, according to the inner imaginative cognition of the artist concerning what was possible at that time in a being that had developed a refractory will. But in any case this form is not to be found among those that became possible in the animal scale up to man in the physical world: it had to remain a supersensible being. But as such it could not exist in the realm inhabited by the beings of the higher hierarchies—angels, archangels, and so forth: it had to be transferred, as it were, placed among the beings that could evolve in the course of physical development. And that is the story of "The Fall of the Dragon from Heaven to Earth". It was Michael's deed, this bestowing of a form that is supra-animalistic: supersensible, but intolerable in the supersensible realm; for although it is supersensible it is incompatible with the realm of the supersensible where it existed before it rebelled.

Thus this form was transferred to the physical world, but as a superphysical, supersensible form. It lived thereafter in the realm where the minerals, plants, and animals live : in what became the earth. But it did not live there in such a way that a human eye could perceive it as it does an ordinary animal. When the soul's eye is raised to those worlds for which provision was made, so to speak, in the plan of higher worlds, it beholds in its imaginations the beings of the higher hierarchies; when the human physical eye observes the physical world it sees simply what has come into being in the various kingdoms of nature, up to the form of the physical-sensible human being. But when the soul's eye is directed to what physical nature embraces, it beholds this inherently contradictory form of the Adversary, of him who is like an animal and yet not like an animal, who dwells in the visible world, yet is himself invisible : it beholds the form of the Dragon. And in the whole genesis of the Dragon men of old saw the act of Michael, who remained in the realm of spirit in the form suitable to that realm.

Now the earth came into being, and with it, man; and it was intended that man should become, in a sense, a twofold being. With one part of his being, with his psycho-spiritual part, he was to reach up into what is called the heavenly, the supersensible world; and with the other, with the physical-etheric part, he was to belong to that nature which came into being as earth-nature, as a new cosmic body—the cosmic body to which the apostate spirit, the Adversary, was relegated. This is where man had to come into being. He was the being who, according to the primordial decree that underlies all, belongs in this world. Man belonged on the earth. The Dragon did not belong on the earth, but he had been transferred thither.

And now consider what man encountered on the earth, as he

6

came into existence with the earth. He encountered what had developed as external nature out of previous nature kingdoms, tending toward and culminating in our present mineral, plant, and animal kingdoms, up to his own physical form. That is what he encountered—in other words, what we are accustomed to call extra-human nature. What was this? It was, and still is today, the perpetuation of what was intended by the highest creative powers in the continuous plan for the world's evolution. That is why the human being, in experiencing it in his *Gemüt*, can look out upon external nature, upon the minerals and all that is connected with the mineral world, upon the wondrous crystal formations—also upon the mountains, the clouds, and all the other forms—and he beholds this outer nature in its condition of death, as it were; of not being alive. But he sees all this that is not alive as something that an earlier divine world discarded—just as the human corpse, though in a different significance, is discarded by the living man at death.

Although the aspect of the human corpse as it appears to us is not primarily anything that can impress us positively, yet that which, in a certain sense, is also a divine corpse, though on a higher plane, and which originated in the mineral kingdom, may be regarded as the factor whose form and shape reflects the originally formless-living divinity. And what then comes into being as the higher kingdoms of nature can be regarded as a further reflection of what originally existed as the formless divine. So man can gaze upon the whole of nature and may feel that this extra-human nature is a mirror of the divine in the world. And after all, that is what nature is intended to give to the human *Gemüt*. Naïvely, and not through speculation, man must be able to feel joy and accord at the sight of this or that manifestation of nature, feel inner jubilation and enthusiasm when he experiences creative nature in its sprouting and blossoming. And his very unawareness of the cause of this elation, this enthusiasm, this overflowing joy in nature—that is what should evoke deep down in his heart the feeling that his *Gemüt* is so intimately related to this nature that he can say to himself—though in dim consciousness: All this the Gods have taken out of themselves and established in the world as their mirror—the same Gods from whom my *Gemüt* derived, from whom I myself sprang by a different way.—And all our inner elation and joy in nature, all that rises in us as a feeling of release when we participate vividly in the freshness of nature, all this should be attuned to the feeling of relationship between our human *Gemüt* and what lives out there in nature as a mirror of Divinity.

As you know, man's position in his evolution is such that he takes nature into himself—takes it in through nourishment, through breathing, and—though in a spiritual way—through perceiving it with his senses. In these three ways external nature enters into man, and it is this that makes him a twofold being. Through his psycho-spiritual being he is related to the beings of the higher hierarchies, but a part of his being he must form out of what he finds in nature. That he takes into himself; and by being received in him as nourishment, as the stimulus of breathing, and even in the more delicate etheric process of perception, it extends in him the processes of outer nature. This appears in him as instinct, passion, animal lust—as everything animalistic that rises out of the depths of his nature. Let us note that carefully. Out there we see wondrously formed crystals, mineral masses that tower into gigantic mountains, fresh mineral forms that flow as water over the earth in the most manifold ways. On a higher plane of formative force we have before us the burgeoning substance and nature of plants, the endless variety of animal forms, and finally the human physical form itself.

All that, living in outer nature, is a mirror of the Godhead. It stands there in its marvellous naïve innocence before the human *Gemüt,* just because it mirrors the Godhead and is at bottom nothing but a pure reflection. Only, one must understand this reflection. Primarily it is not to be comprehended by the in-

8

tellect, but only, as we shall hear in the next lectures, precisely by the *Gemüt*. But if man does understand it with his *Gemüt*—and in the olden times of which I spoke, men did—he sees it as the mirror of the Godhead.—But then he turns to what lives in nature—in the salts, in plants, and in the parts of animals that enter his own body; and he observes what it is that sprouts in the innocent green of the plants and what is even still present in a naïve way in the animal body. All this he now perceives when he looks into himself: he sees it arising in him as passions, as bestial lusts, animal instincts; and he perceives what nature becomes in him.

That was the feeling still cherished by many of the most enlightened men even in the 18th Century. They still felt vividly the difference between outer nature and what nature becomes after man has devoured, breathed, and perceived it. They felt intensely the difference between the naïve outer nature, perceptible to the senses, on the one hand, and human, inwardly surging sensuality, on the other. This difference was still livingly clear to many men who in the 18th Century experienced nature and man and described them to their pupils, described how nature and man are involved in the conflict between Michael and the Dragon.

In considering that this radical contrast still occupied the souls of men in the 18th Century—outer nature in its essential innocence, nature within man in its corruption—we must now recall the Dragon that Michael relegated to this world of nature because he found him unworthy to remain in the world of spirituality. Out there in the world of minerals, plants, even of animals, that Dragon, whose form is incompatible with nature, assumed none of the forms of nature beings. He assumed that dragon form which today must seem fantastic to many of us— a form that must inevitably remain supersensible. It cannot enter a mineral, a plant, or an animal, nor can it enter a physical human body. But it can enter that which outer, innocent nature becomes, in the form of guilt in the welling-up life of instincts in the physical human body. Thus many people as late as the 18th Century said: And the Dragon, the Old Serpent, was cast out of heaven down to the earth, where he had no home; but then he erected his bulwark in the being of man, and now he is entrenched in human nature.

In this way that mighty image of Michael and the Dragon still constituted for those times an integral part of human cognition. An anthroposophy appropriate to that period would have to explain that by taking outer nature into himself through nourishment, breathing, and perception, man creates within himself a sphere of action for the Dragon. The Dragon lives in human nature; and this conception dwelt so definitely in the *Gemüt* of 18th Century men that one could easily imagine them as having stationed some clairvoyant being on another planet to draw a picture of the earth; and he would have shown everything existing in the minerals, plants, and animals—in short, in the extra-human—as bearing no trace of the Dragon, but he would have drawn the Dragon as coiling through the animality in man, thereby representing an earth-being.

Thus the situation had changed for people of the 18th Century from that out of which it all had grown in pre-human times. For pre-humanity the conflict between Michael and the Dragon had to be located in outer objectivity, so to speak; but now the Dragon was outwardly nowhere to be found. Where was he? Where would one have to look for him? Anywhere wherever there were men on earth. That's where he was. If Michael wanted to carry on his mission, which in pre-human times lay in objective nature, when his task was to conquer the Dragon, the world-monster, externally, he must henceforth continue the struggle within human nature.—This occurred in the remote past and persisted into the 18th Century. But those who held this view knew that they had transferred to the inner man an event that had formerly been a cosmic one; and they said, in effect: Look back to olden times when you must imagine Michael to have cast the Dragon out of heaven down to earth—an event taking place in extra-human worlds. And behold the later time: man comes to earth, he takes into himself outer nature, transforms it, thus enabling the Dragon to take possession of it, and the conflict between Michael and the Dragon must henceforth be carried on on the earth.

Such thought trends were not as abstract as people of the present would like thoughts to be. Today people like to get along with thoughts as obvious as possible. They put it this way: Well, formerly an event like the conflict between Michael and the Dragon was simply thought of as external; but during the course of evolution mankind has turned inward, hence such an event is now perceived only inwardly.—Truly, those who are content to stop at such abstractions are not to be envied, and in any case they fail to envision the course of the world history of human thought. For it happened as I have just presented it: the outer cosmic conflict of Michael and the Dragon was transferred to the inner human being, because only in human nature could the Dragon now find his sphere of action.

But precisely this infused into the Michael problem the germinating of human freedom; for if the conflict had continued within man in the same way it had formerly occurred without, the human being would positively have become an automaton. By reason of being transferred to the inner being, the struggle became in a sense—expressed by an outer abstraction—a battle of the higher nature in man against the lower. But the only form it could assume for human consciousness was that of Michael in the supersensible worlds, to which men were led to lift their gaze. And as a matter of fact, in the 18th Century there still existed numerous guides, instructions, all providing ways by which men could reach the sphere of Michael, so that with the help of his strength they might fight the Dragon dwelling in their own animal nature.

Such a man, able to see into the deeper spiritual life of the 18th Century, would have to be represented pictorially somewhat as follows: outwardly the human form; in the lower, animalistic portion the Dragon writhing—even coiling about the heart; but then—behind the man, as it were, for we see the higher things with the back of our head—the outer cosmic figure of Michael, towering, radiant, retaining his cosmic nature but reflecting it in the higher human nature, so that the man's own etheric body reflects etherically the cosmic figure of Michael. Then there would be visible in this human head—but working down into the heart— the power of Michael, crushing the Dragon and causing his blood to flow down from the man's heart to the limbs.

That was the picture of the inner-human struggle of Michael with the Dragon still harbored by many people of the 18th Century. It was also the picture which suggested at that time to many people that it was their duty to conquer the "lower" with the help of the "higher", as they expressed it: that man needed the Michael power for his own life.

The intellect sees the Kant-Laplace theory; it sees the Kant-Laplace primal vapor—perhaps a spiral vapor. Out of this, planets evolve, leaving the sun in the middle. On one of the planets gradually arise the kingdoms of nature; man comes into being. And looking into the future, all this is seen to pass over again into the great graveyard of natural existence.—The intellect cannot help imagining the matter in this way; and because more and more the intellect has become the only recognized autocrat of human cognition, the world view has gradually become what it is for mankind in general. But in all those earlier people of whom I have spoken today the eye of the *Gemüt,* as I might call it, was active. In his intellect a man can isolate himself from the world, for everyone has his own head and in that head his own thoughts. In his *Gemüt* he cannot do that, for the *Gemüt* is not dependent upon the head but upon the rhythmic organism of man. The air I have within me at the present moment, I did not have within me a moment ago: it was the general air; and in another moment it will again be the general air when I exhale it. It is only the head that isolates man, makes of him a hermit on the earth. Even in respect of the physical organization of his *Gemüt*, man is not isolated in this way: in that respect he belongs to the cosmos, is merely a figure in the cosmos.

But gradually the *Gemüt* lost its power of vision, and the head alone became seeing. The head alone, however, develops only intellectuality—it isolates man. When men still saw with their *Gemüt* they did not project abstract thoughts into the cosmos with the object of interpreting it, of explaining it: they still read grandiose images into it,* like that of Michael's Fight with the Dragon. Such a man saw what lived in his own nature and being, something that had evolved out of the world, out of the cosmos, as I described it today. He saw the inner Michael struggle come to life in the human being, in the *anthropos,* and take the place of the external Michael battle in the cosmos. He saw *anthroposophy* develop out of *cosmosophy.* And whenever we look back to an older world view from the abstract thoughts that affect us as cold and matter-of-fact, whose intellectuality makes us shiver, we are guided to images one of the most grandiose of which is this of Michael at war with the Dragon; Michael, who first cast the Dragon to earth where, I might say, the Dragon could occupy his human fortress; Michael, who then became the fighter of the Dragon in man, as described.

In this picture that I have evoked for you, Michael stands cosmically behind man, while within man there is an etheric image of Michael that wages the real battle through which man can gradually become free; for it is not Michael himself who wages the battle, but human devotion and the resulting image of Michael. In the cosmic Michael there still lives that being to whom

---

*Translator's Note: "Saw" them into it, is Rudolf Steiner's expression.

men can look up and who engaged in the original cosmic struggle with the Dragon. Truly, not upon earth alone do events take place—in fact, earth events remain incomprehensible for us unless we are able to see them as images of events in the supersensible world and to find their causes there. In this sense a Michael deed was performed in the supersensible realm shortly before our time, a deed I should like to characterize in the following way. In doing so I must speak in a manner that is nowadays discredited as anthropomorphic; but how could I relate it otherwise than by using human words to describe what occurs in the supersensible world?

The epoch during which Michael cast the Dragon down to earth was thought of as lying far back in pre-human times; but then, man appeared upon the earth and there occurred what I have described: the war between Michael and the Dragon became ever more an inner struggle. It was at the end of the 19th Century that Michael could say: The image in man is now sufficiently condensed for him to be aware of it within himself: he can now feel in his *Gemüt* the Conqueror of the Dragon—at least, the image means something to him.—In the evolution of mankind the last third of the 19th Century stands for something extraordinarily important. In older times there was in man primarily only a tenuous image of Michael; but it condensed more and more, and in the last third of the 19th Century there appeared what follows: In earlier times the invisible, supersensible Dragon was predominant, active in the passions and instincts, in the desires and in the animal lusts. For ordinary consciousness that Dragon remains subsensible; he dwells in man's animal nature. But there he lives in all that tends to drag man down, goading him into becoming gradually sub-human. The condition was such that Michael always intervened in human nature, in order that humanity should not fall too low.

But in the last third of the 19th Century the Michael image became so strong in man that the matter of directing his feelings upward and rising to the Michael image came to depend upon his good-will, so to speak; so that on the one hand, in unenlightened experience of the feelings, he may glimpse the image of the Dragon, and on the other hand, the radiant figure of Michael may stand before the soul's eye—radiant in spiritual vision, yet within the reach of ordinary consciousness. So the content of the human *Gemüt* can be this: The power of the Dragon is working within me, trying to drag me down. I do not see it— I *feel* it as something that would drag me down below myself. But in the spirit I *see* the luminous Angel whose cosmic task has always been the vanquishing of the Dragon. I concentrate my *Gemüt* upon this glowing figure, I let its light stream into my *Gemüt*, and thus my illumined and warmed *Gemüt* will bear within it the strength of Michael. And out of a free resolution I shall be able, through my alliance with Michael, to conquer the Dragon's might in my own lower nature.

If the requisite good-will were forthcoming in extensive circles to raise such a conception to a religious force and to inscribe it in every *Gemüt*, we would not have all the vague and impotent ideas such as prevail in every quarter today—plans for reforms, and the like. Rather we would have something that once again could seize hold on the whole inner man, because that is what can be inscribed in the living *Gemüt*—that living *Gemüt* which enters into a living relationship with the whole cosmos the moment it really comes to life.

Then those glowing Michael thoughts would be the first harbingers of our ability to penetrate once more into the supersensible world. The striving for enlightenment would become inwardly and deeply religious. And thereby men would be prepared for the festivals of the year, the understanding of which only glimmers faintly across the ages—but at least it glimmers— and they would celebrate in full consciousness the festival the calendar sets at the end of September, at the beginning of autumn: the Michael Festival. This will regain its significance only when we are able to experience in our soul such a living vision. And when we are able to feel it in a living way and to make it into an instinctive social impulse of the present, then this Michael Festival—because the impulses spring directly from the spiritual world—could be regarded as the crowning impulse— even the initial impulse we need to find our way out of the present disaster; to add something real to all the talk about ideals, something not originating in human heads or hearts but in the cosmos.

And then, when the trees shed their leaves and blossoms ripen into fruit, when nature sends us her first frost and prepares to sink into her winter death, we would be able to feel the burgeoning of spirit with which we should unite ourself—just as we feel the Easter Festival with the sprouting, budding spring. Then, as citizens of the cosmos, we would be able to carry impulses into our lives which, not being abstract, would not remain ineffectual but would manifest their power immediately. Life will not have a soul content again until we can develop cosmic impulses in our *Gemüt*.

II

YOU will have sensed, my dear friends, in what I was able to tell you at the close of yesterday's lecture, concerning the old conceptions of Michael's conflict with the Dragon, an indication that for our time a revitalization is called for of the elements of a *Weltanschauung* once contained for mankind in this gigantic picture—and not even so long ago. I repeatedly drew attention to the fact that in many 18th Century souls this conception was still fully alive. But before I can tell you—as I shall in the next lectures—what a genuine, up-to-date spiritual viewpoint can and must do to revivify it, I must present to you— episodically, as it were—a more general anthroposophical train of thought. This will disclose the way in which the conception under discussion can be revitalized and once more become a force in mankind's thinking, feeling, and acting.

If we observe our present relation to nature and to the whole world, and if we compare this with sufficient openmindedness with that of former times, we find that at bottom man has become a veritable hermit in his attitude toward the cosmic powers, a hermit in so far as he is introduced through his birth into physical existence and has lost the memory of his prenatal life— a memory that at one time was common to all mankind. During that period of our life in which nowadays we merely grow into the use of our forces of mind and memory, and to which we can remember back in this earth life, there occurred in former epochs of human evolution the lighting up of real memory, of an actual retrospect of prenatal experiences man had passed through as a psycho-spiritual being before his earth life.—That is one factor that makes present-day man a world-hermit: he is not conscious of the nature of the connection between his earthly existence and his spiritual existence.

The other factor is this: when now he gazes into the vast cosmos he observes the outer forms of the stars and constellations, but he no longer has any inner spiritual relation to what is spiritual in the cosmos. We can go further: the man of today observes the kingdoms of nature that surround him on earth—the manifold beauty of plants, the gigantic proportions of mountains, the fleeting clouds, and so on. Yet here again he is limited to sense impressions; and often he is even afraid, when he feels a deeper, more intimate contact with the great spaces of nature, lest he might lose his ingenuous attitude toward them. This phase of human evolution was indispensable for the development of what we experience in the consciousness of freedom, the feeling of freedom, in order to arrive at full self-consciousness, at the inner strength that permits the ego to rise to its full height; but necessary as was this hermit life of man in relation to the cosmos, it must be but a transition to another epoch in which the human being may find the way back to spirit, which after all underlies all things and beings. And precisely this finding the way back to spirit must be achieved by means of the strength that can come to him who is able to grasp the Michael idea in its right sense and in its true form, the form it must assume in our time.

Our mentality, the life of our *Gemüt,* and our life of action all need to be permeated with the Michael impulse. But when we hear it stated that a Michael Festival must be resuscitated among men and that the time is ripe for assigning it its place among the other annual festivals, it is naturally not enough that a few people should say, Well let us start—let us have a Michael Festival! My dear friends, if anthroposophy is to achieve its aim, the superficiality so prevalent today must obviously play no part in any anthroposophical undertakings; but rather, whatever may grow out of anthroposophy must do so with the most profound seriousness. And in order to familiarize ourselves with what this seriousness should be we must consider in what manner the

18

festivals—once vital, today so anaemic—took their place in human evolution. Did the Christmas or the Easter Festival come into being because a few people had the idea of instituting a festival at a certain time of the year and said, Let us make the necessary arrangements? Naturally that is not the case. For something like the Christmas Festival to find its way into the life of mankind, Christ Jesus had to be born: this event had to enter the world-historical evolution of the earth; a transcendent event had to occur. And the Easter Festival? It could never have had any meaning in the world had it not commemorated what took place through the Mystery of Golgotha, had not this event intervened incisively for the history of the earth in the evolution of humanity. If nowadays these festivals have faded, if the whole seriousness of the Christmas and Easter Festivals is no longer felt, this fact in itself should lead to a revived intensification of them through a more profound comprehension of the birth of Christ Jesus and the Mystery of Golgotha. Under no conditions, however, must it be imagined that one should add to these festivals simply by establishing a Michael Festival with equal superficiality at the beginning of autumn. Something must be present that can be incisive in human evolution in the same way—though possibly to a lesser degree—as were all events that led to the institution of festivals.

The possibility of celebrating a Michael Festival in all seriousness must inevitably be brought about, and it is the anthroposophical movement out of which an understanding for such a Michael Festival must be able to arise. But just as the Christmas and Easter Festivals were led up to by outer events, in evolutionary objectivity, so a radical transformation must take place in the inner being of mankind before such a step is taken. Anthroposophy must become a profound experience, an experience men can think of in a way similar to that which they feel when imbued with the whole power dwelling in the birth of Christ Jesus, in the Mystery of Golgotha. As was said, this may be so to a lesser degree in the case of the Michael Festival; but something of this soul-transmuting force must proceed from the anthroposophical movement. That is indeed what we long for: that anthroposophy might be imbued with this power to transmute souls; and this can only come about if the substance of its teaching—if I may call it that—becomes actual experience.

Let us now turn our attention to such experiences as can enter our inner being through anthroposophy. In our soul life we distinguish, as you know, thinking, feeling, and willing from one another; and especially in connection with feeling we speak of the human *Gemüt*. Our thinking appears to us cold, dry, colorless — as though spiritually emaciating us — when our thoughts take an abstract form, when we are unable to imbue them with the warmth and enthusiasm of feeling. We can call a man *gemütvoll* only when something of the inner warmth of his *Gemüt* streams forth to us when he utters his thoughts. And we can really make close contact with a man only if his behavior toward ourself and the world is not merely correct and in line with duty, but if his actions manifest enthusiasm, a warm heart, a love of nature, love for every being. This human *Gemüt*, then, dwells in the very center of the soul life, as it were.

But while thinking and willing have assumed a certain character by reason of man's having become cosmically a hermit, this is even more true of the human *Gemüt*. Thinking may contemplate the perfection of its cosmic calculations and perhaps gloat over their subtlety, but it simply fails to sense how basically remote it is from the warm heartbeat of life. And in correct actions, carried out by a mere sense of duty, many a man may find satisfaction, without really feeling that a life of such matter-of-fact behavior is but half a life. Neither the one nor the other touches the human soul very closely. But what lies between thinking and willing, all that is comprised in the human *Gemüt*, is indeed intimately linked with the whole being of man. And while it may sometimes seem—in view of the peculiar tendencies

20

of many people at the present time—as though the factors that should warm and elevate the *Gemüt* and fill it with enthusiasm might become chilled as well, this is a delusion. For it can be said that a man's inner, conscious experiences might at a pinch occur lacking the element of *Gemüt;* but through such a lack his being will inevitably suffer in some way. And if such a man's soul can endure this—if perhaps through soullessness he forces himself to *Gemüt*lessness—the process will gnaw at his whole being in some other form: it will eat right down into his physical organization, affecting his health. Much of what appears in our time as symptoms of decline is basically connected with the lack of *Gemüt* into which many people have settled.—The full import of these rather general statements will become clear when we delve deeper into them.

One who simply grows up into our modern civilization observes the things of the outer world: he perceives them, forms abstract thoughts about them, possibly derives real pleasure from a lovely blossom or a majestic plant; and if he is at all imaginative he may even achieve an inner picture of these. Yet he remains completely unaware of his deeper relation to that world of which the plant, for example, is a part. To talk incessantly about spirit, spirit, and again spirit is utterly inadequate for spiritual perception. Instead, what is needed is that we should become conscious of our true spiritual relations to the things around us. When we observe a plant in the usual way we do not in the least sense the presence of an elemental being dwelling in it, of something spiritual; we do not dream that every such plant harbors something which is not satisfied by having us look at it and form such abstract mental pictures as we commonly do of plants today. For in every plant there is concealed—under a spell, as it were—an elemental spiritual being; and really only he observes a plant in the right way who realizes that this loveliness is the sheath of a spiritual being enchanted in it—a relatively insignificant being, to be sure, in the great scale of cosmic interrelationships, but still a being intimately related to man.

The human being is really so closely linked to the world that he cannot take a step in the realm of nature without coming under the intense influence exercised upon him by his intimate relations to the world. And when we see the lily in the field, growing from the seed to the blossom, we must vividly imagine—though not personified—that this lily is awaiting something. (Again I must use men's words as I did before to express another picture: they cannot quite cover the meaning, but they do express the realities inherent in things.) While unfolding its leaves, but especially its blossom, this lily is really expecting something. It says to itself: Men will pass and look at me; and when a sufficient number of human eyes will have directed their gaze upon me—so speaks the spirit of the lily—I shall be disenchanted of my spell, and I shall be able to start on my way into spiritual worlds.—You will perhaps object that many lilies grow unseen by human eye: yes, but then the conditions are different, and such lilies find their release in a different way. For the decree that the spell of that particular lily shall be broken by human eyes comes about by the first human glance cast upon the lily. It is a relationship entered into between man and the lily when he first lets his gaze rest upon it.—All about us are these elemental spirits begging us, in effect, Do not look at the flowers so abstractly, nor form such abstract mental pictures of them: let rather your heart and your *Gemüt* enter into what lives, as soul and spirit, in the flowers, for it is imploring you to break the spell.—Human existence should really be a perpetual releasing of the elemental spirits lying enchanted in minerals, plants, and animals.

An idea such as this can readily be sensed in its abundant beauty; but precisely by grasping it in its right spiritual significance we can also feel it in the light of the full responsibility we thereby incur toward the whole cosmos. In the present epoch

22

of civilization—that of the development of freedom—man's attitude toward the flowers is a mere sipping at what he should really be drinking. He sips by forming concepts and ideas, whereas he should drink by uniting, through his *Gemüt,* with the elemental spirits of the things and beings that surround him.

I said, we need not consider the lilies that are never seen by man but must think of those that are so seen, because they need the relationship of the *Gemüt* which the human being can enter into with them. Now, it is from the lily that an effect proceeds; and manifold, mighty and magnificent are indeed the spiritual effects that continually approach man out of the things of nature when he walks in it. One who can see into these things constantly perceives the variety and grandeur of all that streams out to him from all sides through the elemental spirituality of nature. And it flows into him: it is something that constantly streams toward him as supersensible spirituality poured out over outer nature, which is a mirror of the divine-spiritual.

In the next days we shall have occasion to speak of these matters more in detail, in the true anthroposophical sense. At the moment we will go on to say that in the human being there dwells the force I have described as the force of the Dragon whom Michael encounters, against whom he does battle. I indicated that this Dragon has an animal-like form, yet is really a supersensible being; that on account of his insubordination as a supersensible being he was expelled into the sense world, where he now has his being; and I indicated further that he exists only in man, because outer nature cannot harbor him. Outer nature, image of divine spirituality, has in its innocence nothing whatever to do with the Dragon: he is established in the being of men, as I have set forth. But by reason of being such a creature —a supersensible being in the sense world—he instantly attracts the supersensible elemental forces that stream toward man out of nature and unites with them, with the result that man, instead of releasing the plant elementals from their spell through his soul and *Gemüt,* unites them with the Dragon, allows them to perish with the Dragon in his lower nature. For everything in the world moves in an evolutionary stream, taking many different directions to this end; and the elemental beings dwelling in minerals, plants, and animals must rise to a higher existence than is offered by their present abodes. This they can only accomplish by passing through man. The establishment of an external civilization is surely not man's sole purpose on earth: he has a cosmic aim within the entire world evolution; and this cosmic aim is linked with such matters as I have just described—with the further development of those elemental beings that in earthly existence are at a low stage, but destined for a higher one. When man enters into a certain relationship with them, and when everything runs as it should, they can attain to this higher stage of evolution.

In the old days of instinctive human evolution, when in the *Gemüt* the forces of soul and spirit shone forth and when these were as much a matter of course to him as were the forces of nature, world evolution actually progressed in such a way that the stream of existence passed through man in a normal, orderly way, as it were. But precisely during the epoch that must now terminate, that must advance to a higher form of spirituality, untold elemental substance within man has been delivered over to the Dragon; for it is his very nature to hunger and thirst for these elemental beings: to creep about, frightening plants and minerals in order to gorge himself with the elemental beings of nature. For with them he wants to unite, and with them to permeate his own being. In extrahuman nature he cannot do this, but only in the inner nature of man, for only there is existence possible for him. And if this were to continue, the earth would be doomed, for the Dragon would inevitably be victorious in earthly existence.

He would be victorious for a very definite reason: by virtue of his saturating himself, as it were, with elemental beings in

24

human nature, something happens physically, psychically, and spiritually. Spiritually: no human being would ever arrive at the silly belief in a purely material outer world, as assumed by nature research today; he would never come to accept dead atoms and the like; he would never assume the existence of such reactionary laws as that of the conservation of force and energy, or of the permanence of matter, were not the Dragon in him to absorb the elemental beings from without. When these come to be in man, in the body of the Dragon, human observation is distracted from what things contain of spirit: man no longer sees spirit in things, which in the meantime has entered into him; he sees nothing but dead matter.—Psychically: everything a man has ever expressed in the way of what I must call cowardice of soul results from the Dragon's having absorbed the elemental powers within him. Oh, how widespread is this cowardice of the soul! We know quite well that we should do this or that, that such and such is the right thing to do in a given situation; but we cannot bring ourself to do it—a certain dead weight acts in our soul: the elemental beings in the Dragon's body are at work in us.—And physically: man would never be tormented by what are called disease germs had his body not been prepared —through the spiritual effects I have just described—as a soil for the germs. These things penetrate even into the physical organization; and we can say that if we perceive man rightly in his spirit, soul, and body as he is constituted today, we find him cut off from the spirit realm in three directions—for a good purpose, to be sure: the attainment of freedom. He no longer has in him the spiritual powers he might have; and thus you see that through this threefold debilitation of his life, through what the glutted Dragon has become in him, he is prevented from experiencing the potency of the spirit within himself.

There are two ways of experiencing anthroposophy—many variations lie between, but I am mentioning only the two extremes—and one of them is this: a man sits down in a chair, takes a book, reads it, and finds it quite interesting as well as comforting to learn that there is such a thing as spirit, as immortality. It just suits him to know that with regard to the soul as well, man is not dead when his body dies. He derives greater satisfaction from such a cosmogony than from a materialistic one. He takes it up as one might take up abstract reflections on geography, except that anthroposophy provides more of comfort. Yes, that is one way. The man gets up from his chair really no different from what he was when he sat down, except for having derived a certain satisfaction from what he read— or heard, if it was a lecture instead of a book.

But there is another way of receiving what anthroposophy has to give. It is to absorb something like the idea of Michael's Conflict with the Dragon in such a way as really to become inwardly transformed, to feel it as an important, incisive experience, and to rise from your chair fundamentally quite a different being after reading something of that sort.—And as has been said, there are all sorts of shades between these two.

The first type of reader cannot be counted upon at all when it is a question of reviving the Michaelmas Festival: only those can be depended upon whose determination it is, at least within their capacities, to take anthroposophy into themselves as something living. And that is exactly what should be experienced within the anthroposophical movement: the need to experience as life-forces those ideas that first present themselves to us merely as such, as ideas.—Now I will say something wholly paradoxical: sometimes it is much easier to understand the opponents of anthroposophy than its adherents. The opponents say, Oh, these anthroposophical ideas are fantastic—they conform with no reality; and they reject them, remain untouched by them. One can readily understand such an attitude and find a variety of reasons for it. As a rule it is caused by fear of these ideas—a real attitude, though unconscious. But frequently it happens that a man accepts the ideas; yet, though they diverge so radically from everything else in the world that can be accepted, they produce less feeling in him than would an electrifying apparatus applied to his knuckle. In the latter case he at least feels in his body a twitching produced by the spark; and the absence of a similar spark in the soul is what so often causes great anguish. —This links up with the demand of our time that men be laid hold of and impressed by the spirit, not merely by what is physical. Men avoid being knocked and jerked about, but they do not avoid coming in contact with ideas dealing with other worlds, ideas presenting themselves as something very special in the present-day sense-world, and then maintaining the same indifference toward them as toward ideas of the senses.

This ability to rise to the point at which thoughts about spirit can grip us as powerfully as can anything in the physical world, this is Michael power. It is confidence in the ideas of spirit— given the capacity for receiving them at all—leading to the conviction: I have received a spiritual impulse, I give myself up to it, I become the instrument for its execution. First failure— never mind! Second failure—never mind! A hundred failures are of no consequence, for no failure is ever a decisive factor in judging the truth of a spiritual impulse whose effect has been inwardly understood and grasped. We have full confidence in a spiritual impulse, grasped at a certain point of time, only when we can say to ourself, My hundred failures can at most prove that the conditions for realizing the impulse are not given me in this incarnation; but that this impulse is right I can know from its own nature. And if I must wait a hundred incarnations for the power to realize this impulse, nothing but its own nature can convince me of the efficacy or impotence of any spiritual impulse.

If you will imagine this thought developed in the human *Gemüt* as great confidence in spirit, if you will consider that man can cling firm as a rock to something he has seen to be spiritually victorious, something he refuses to relinquish in spite of all outer opposition, then you will have a conception of what the

Michael power, the Michael being, really demands of us; for only then will you comprehend the nature of the great confidence in spirit. We may leave in abeyance some spiritual impulse or other, even for a whole incarnation; but once we have grasped it we must never waver in cherishing it within us, for only thus can we save it up for subsequent incarnations. And when confidence in spirit will in this way have established a frame of mind to which this spiritual substance appears as real as the ground under our feet—the ground without which we could not stand —then we shall have in our *Gemüt* a feeling of what Michael really expects of us.

Undoubtedly you will admit that in the course of the last centuries—even the last thousand years of human history—the vastly greater part of this active confidence in spirit has been disappearing, that life does not exact from the majority of men the development of such confidence. Yet that is what had to come, because what I am really expressing when I say this is that in the last instance man has burned the bridges that formerly had communication with the Michael power.

But in the meantime much has happened in the world. Man has in a sense apostatized from the Michael power. The stark, intense materialism of the 19th Century is in effect an apostasy from the Michael power. But objectively, in the domain of outer spirit, the Michael power has been victorious, precisely in the last third of the 19th Century. What the Dragon had hoped to achieve through human evolution will not come to pass, yet on the other hand we envision today the other great fact that out of free resolution man will have to take part in Michael's victory over the Dragon. And this involves finding the way to abandon the prevalent passivity in relation to spirit and to enter into an active one. The Michael forces cannot be acquired through any form of passivity, not even through passive prayer, but only through man's making himself the instrument of divine-spiritual forces by means of his loving will. *For the Michael forces do not want to be implored: they want men to unite with them. This men can do if they will receive the lessons of the spiritual world with inner energy.*

This will indicate what must appear in man if the Michael conception is to come alive again. He must really be able to experience spirit, and he must be able to gather this experience wholly out of thought—not in the first instance by means of some sort of clairvoyance. We would be in a bad way if everybody had to become clairvoyant in order to have this confidence in spirit. Everyone who is at all receptive to the teachings of spiritual science can have this confidence. If a man will saturate himself more and more with confidence in spirit, something will come over him like an inspiration; and this is something that really all the good spirits of the world are awaiting. He will experience the spring, sensing the beauty and loveliness of the plant world and finding deep delight in the sprouting, burgeoning life; but at the same time he will develop a feeling for the spellbound elemental spirituality in all this budding life. He will acquire a feeling, a *Gemüt* content, telling him that every blossom bears testimony to the existence of an enchanted elemental being within it; and he will learn to feel the longing in this elemental being to be released by him, instead of being delivered up to the Dragon to whom it is related through its own invisibility. And when the flowers wither in the autumn, he will know that he has succeeded in contributing a bit to the progress of spirit in the world, in enabling an elemental being to slip out of its plant when the blossoms wither and fall and become seed. But only as he has permeated himself with the powerful strength of Michael will he be able to lead this elemental being up into the spirit for which it yearns.

And men will experience the cycle of the seasons. They will experience spring as the birth of elemental beings longing for the spirit, and autumn as their liberation from the dying plants and withering blossoms. They will no longer stand alone as cosmic hermits who have merely grown half a year older by fall than they were in the spring: together with evolving nature they will have pressed onward by one of life's milestones. They will not merely have inhaled the physical oxygen so and so many times, but will have participated in the evolution of nature, in the enchanting and disenchanting of spiritual beings in nature. Men will no longer only feel themselves growing older; they will sense the transformation of nature as part of their own destiny: they will coalesce with all that grows there, will expand in their being because their free individuality can pour itself out in sacrifice into the cosmos.—That is what man will be able to contribute to a favorable outcome of Michael's Conflict with the Dragon.

Thus we see that what can lead to a Michaelmas Festival must be an event of the human *Gemüt,* a *Gemüt* event that can once more experience the cycle of the seasons as a living reality, in the manner described. But do not imagine you are experiencing it by merely setting up this abstract concept in your mind! You will achieve this only after you have actually absorbed anthroposophy in such a way that it makes you regard every plant, every stone, in a new way; and also, only after anthroposophy has taught you to contemplate all human life in a new way.

I have tried to give you a sort of picture of what must be prepared specifically in the human *Gemüt,* if the latter is to learn to feel surrounding nature as its very own being. The most that men have retained of this sort of thing is the ability to experience in their blood circulation a certain psychic element in addition to the material factor: unless they are rank materialists they have preserved that much. But to experience the pulsebeat of outer existence as we do our own innermost being, to take part once more in the cycle of the seasons as we experience the life inside our own skin—that is the preparation needed for the Michael Festival.

Inasmuch as these lectures are intended to present for your

contemplation the relation between anthroposophy and the human *Gemüt,* it is my wish that they may really be grasped not merely by the head but especially by the *Gemüt;* for at bottom, all anthroposophy is largely futile in the world and among men if it is not absorbed by the *Gemüt,* if it carries no warmth into this human *Gemüt.* Recent centuries have heaped cleverness in abundance upon men: in the matter of thinking, men have come to the point where they no longer even know how clever they are. That is a fact. True, many people believe present-day men to be stupid; but granting that there are stupid people in the world, this is really only because their cleverness has reached such proportions that the debility of their *Gemüt* prevents them from knowing what to do with all their cleverness. Whenever someone is called stupid, I always maintain that it is merely a case of his not knowing what use to make of his cleverness. I have listened to many discussions in which some speaker or other was ridiculed because he was considered stupid, but occasionally just one of these would seem to me the cleverest.

Cleverness, then, has been furnished us in abundance by the last few centuries; but what we need today is warmth of *Gemüt,* and this anthroposophy can provide. When someone studying anthroposophy says it leaves him cold, he reminds me of one who keeps piling wood in the stove and then complains that the room doesn't get warm. Yet all he needs to do is to kindle the wood, then it will get warm. Anthroposophy can be presented, and it is the good wood of the soul; but it can be enkindled only by each within himself. What everyone must find in his *Gemüt* is the match wherewith to light anthroposophy. Anthroposophy is in truth warm and ardent: it is the very soul of the *Gemüt;* and he who finds this anthroposophy cold and intellectual and matter-of-fact just lacks the means of kindling it so it may pervade him with its fire. And just as only a little match is needed to light ordinary wood, so anthroposophy, too, needs only a little match. But this will enkindle the force of Michael in man.

III

IN the first of these lectures I endeavored to set forth how Michael's Conflict with the Dragon persisted into the 18th Century as a determining idea, really a determining impulse in mankind; and in the second lecture I tried to show how a productive revival of this impulse may and really must be brought about. But now, before discussing particulars for a Michael Festival at the beginning of autumn, I should like today to speak about several prerequisites involved in such an intention.

The core of the matter is this: all impulses such as the Michael impulse depend upon man's attaining to supersensible enlightenment concerning his connection not only with earthly but with cosmic conditions: he must learn to feel himself not only as an earth citizen but as a citizen of the universe, as far as this is perceptible either spiritually or, in image, physically. Nowadays, of course, our general education offers only the most meager opportunities for sensing our connection with the cosmos. True, by means of their materialistically colored science men are aware of earth conditions to the point of feeling connected with them, at least as regards their material life in the wider sense. But the knowledge of this connection certainly engenders no enthusiasm, hence all outer signs of such a connection have become very dim. Human feeling for the traditional festivals has grown dim and shadowy. While in former periods of human evolution festivals like Christmas or Easter exerted a far-reaching influence on the entire social life and its manifestations, they have become but a faint echo of what they once meant, expressing themselves in all sorts of customs that lack all deeper social significance.

Now, if we intend in some way to realize the Michael Festival with its particularly far-reaching social significance, we must naturally first create a feeling for what it might signify; for by no means must it bear the character of our modern festivities, but should be brought forth from the depths of the human being. These depths we can only reach by once more penetrating and entering into our relationship with the extra-terrestrial cosmos and with what this yields for the cycle of the seasons.

To illustrate what I really mean by all that, I need only ask you to consider how abstract, how dreadfully out of touch with the human being, are all the feelings and conceptions of the extra-terrestrial universe that today enter human consciousness. Think of what astronomy, astro-physics, and other related sciences accomplish today. They compute the paths of the planets —the positions of the fixed stars, if you like; and from the results of research in spectral analysis they arrive at conclusions concerning the material composition of these heavenly bodies. But what have all the results of such methods to do with the intimate inner soul life of man? This man, equipped with all such sky-wisdom, feels himself a hermit on what he thinks of as the planet earth. And the present habits of thinking connected with these matters are at bottom only a system of very circumscribed concepts.

To get a better light on this, let us consider a condition of consciousness certainly present in ordinary life, though an inferior one: the condition of dream-pervaded sleep. In order to obtain points of contact for today's discussion I will tell you in a few words what relates to this condition. Dreaming may be associated with inner conditions of the human organism and transform these into pictures resembling symbols *—the movements of the heart, for example, can be symbolized by flames, and so forth: we can determine concretely and in detail the connection between dream symbols and our inner organic states and proc-

---

*See: Rudolf Steiner, *Supersensible Knowledge* (*Anthroposophy*) *as a Demand of the Age; Anthroposophy and the Ethical-Religious Conduct of Life,* Anthroposophic Press, New York.

esses. Or alternatively, outer events of our life may be symbolized, events that have remained in us as memories or the like. In any case it is misleading to take the conceptional content of a dream very seriously. This can be interesting, it has a sensational aspect, it is of great interest to many people; but for those who see deeper into the nature of man the dream content as it pertains to the conception proper is of extraordinarily little significance. The dramatic development of a dream, on the other hand, is of the greatest import. I will illustrate this:

Suppose a man dreams he is climbing a mountain. It is an excessively difficult climb and becomes ever more so, the higher he goes. Finally he reaches a point where his strength fails him and conditions have become so unfavorable that he cannot proceed: he must come to a halt. Something like fear, something of disappointment enters his dream. Perhaps at this point he wakes up.—Now, something underlies this dream that should really not be sought in the pictures themselves as they appeal to the imagination, but rather in the emotional experiencing of an intention, in the increasingly formidable obstructions appearing in the path of this intention, and in the circumstance of encountering even more insuperable obstacles. If we think of all that as proceeding in an emotional-dramatic way we discover a certain emotional content underlying the actual dream pictures as dramatic content.—This same emotional content could give rise to quite a different dream. The man might dream he is entering a cave. It gets darker and darker as he gropes along until he finally comes to a swamp. There he wades a bit farther, but finally arrives at a quagmire that stops further progress. This picture embraces the same emotional and sentient dramatic content as the other; and the dramatic content in question could be dreamt in still many other forms.

The pictorial content of a dream may vary continually; the essential factor is what underlies the dream in the way of movements, tension and relaxation, hope and disappointment. Never-

34

theless, the dream presents itself in pictures, and we must ask, How do these arise? They do so, for example, because at the moment of awaking something is experienced by the ego and astral body outside the physical and etheric bodies. The nature of such supersensible experiences is of course something that cannot possibly be expressed in pictures borrowed from the sense world; but as the ego and the astral body reunite with the physical and etheric bodies they have no choice but to use pictures from the available supply. In this way the peculiar dream drama is clothed in pictures.

Now we begin to take an interest in the content of these pictures. Their conformation is entirely different from that of other experiences. Why? Our dreams employ nothing but outer or inner experiences, but they give these a different contiguity. Why is this? It is because dreams are a protest against our mode of life in the physical sense-world during our waking hours. There we live wholly interwoven with the system of natural laws, and dreams break through this. Dreams will not stand for it, so they rip events out of their context and present them in another sequence. They protest against the system of natural laws—in fact, men should learn that every immersion into spirit is just such a protest.

In this connection, there are certain quaint people who keep trying to penetrate the spiritual world by means of the ordinary natural-scientific method. Extraordinarily interesting in this connection is Dr. Ludwig Staudenmaier's book on *Experimental Magic*. A man of that type starts with the assumption that everything which is to be comprehended should be comprehended according to the natural-scientific mode of thought. Now, Staudenmaier does not exactly occupy himself with dreams as such but with so-called mediumistic phenomena, which are really an extension of the dream world. In healthy human beings the dream remains an experience that does not pass over into the outer organization; whereas in the case of a medium everything that is ordinarily experienced by the ego and the astral body, and that then takes shape in the pictures provided by the physical and etheric bodies, passes over into the experiences of the physical and etheric bodies. This is what gives rise to all the phenomena associated with mediumistic conditions.—Staudenmaier was quite right in refusing to be guided by what other mediums offered him, so he set about making himself into a sort of medium. He dreamt while writing, so to speak: he applied the pencil as he had seen mediums do it, and sure enough, it worked! But he was greatly astonished at what came to light: he was amazed at sequences he had never thought of. He wrote all sorts of things wholly foreign to the realm of his conscious life. What he had written was frequently so remote from his conscious life that he asked, "Who is writing this?" And the answer came, "Spirits". He had to write "spirits"! Imagine: the materialist, who of course recognizes no spirits, had to write down "spirits". But he was convinced that whatever was writing through him was lying, so he asked next why the spirits lied to him so; and they said, "Well, we have to lie to you—that is our way." Then he asked about all sorts of things that concerned himself, and once they went so far as to say "muttonhead".* Now, we cannot assume his frame of mind to have been such as to make him label himself a muttonhead. But in any case, all sorts of things came to light that were summed up in the phrase, "we have to lie to you"; so he reflected that since there are naturally no spirits, his subconscious mind must be speaking. But now the case becomes still more alarming: the subconscious calls the conscious mind a muttonhead, and it lies; hence this personality would have to confess, "In my subconscious mind I am an unqualified liar."

But ultimately all this merely points to the fact that the world into which the medium plunges down registers a protest against the constraint of the laws of nature, exactly as does the world

---

*Kohlkopf—literally "cabbage-head".

of dreams. Everything we can think, will, or feel in the physical sense-world is distorted the moment we enter this more or less subconscious world. Why? Well, dreams are the bridge leading to the spiritual world, and the spiritual world is wholly permeated by a set of laws that are not the laws of nature, but laws that bear an entirely different inner character. Dreams are the transition to this world. It is a grave error to imagine that the spiritual world can be comprehended by means of natural laws; and dreams are the herald, as it were, warning us of the impossibility of merely extending the laws of nature when we penetrate into the spiritual world. The same *methods* can be carried over if we prepare ourselves to accomplish this; but in penetrating into the spiritual world we enter an entirely different system of *laws*.

The idea that the world can and should be comprehended only by means of the mental capacities developed in the course of the last three or four hundred years has today become an axiom. This has come about gradually. Today there are no longer such men as were still to be found in the first half of the 19th Century, men, for example, of the type of Johannes Müller, Haeckel's teacher, who confessed that many a bit of research he was carrying on purely as a physiologist refused to be clarified as long as he thought about it in his ordinary waking condition, but that subsequently a dream had brought back to him the whole work of preparing the tissue when awake, all the steps he had taken, and thus many such riddles were solved in his dreams. And Johannes Müller was also one of those who were still fully convinced that in sleep a man dwells in this peculiar spiritual weaving, untouched by inexorable natural laws; where one can even penetrate into the system of physical nature laws, because underlying these there is again something spiritual, and because what is spiritual is fundamentally not subject to natural necessity but merely manifests this on the visible surface.

One really has to speak in paradoxes if thoughts that result quite naturally from spiritual research are to be carried to their logical conclusion. No one who thinks in line with modern natural science believes that a light shining at a given point in space will appear equally bright at a distance. The physicist computes the decrease in the strength of light by the square of the distance, and he calculates gravity in the same way. Regarding these physical entities, he knows that the validity of what is true on the earth's surface diminishes as we pass out into the surrounding cosmos. But he refuses to apply this principle to his thinking. Yet in this respect thinking differs in no way from anything we can learn about earth matters in the laboratories, in the operating rooms—from anything on earth, right down to twice two is four. If gravity diminishes by the square of the distance, why should not the validity of the system of nature laws diminish in a similar ratio and eventually, beyond a certain distance, cease altogether?

That is where spiritual science penetrates. It points out that when the Nebula of Orion or the Canes Nebula is to be the subject of research, the same course is followed as though, with tellurian concepts, Venus, for example, were to be illuminated by the flame of a candle. When spiritual science reveals the truth by means of such analogies people think it is paradoxical. Nevertheless, in the state in which during sleep we penetrate into the spiritual world, greater possibilities are offered us for investigating the Nebula of Orion or the Canes Nebula than are provided by working in laboratories or in observatories. Research would yield much more if we *dreamt* about these matters instead of reflecting on them with our intellect. As soon as we enter the cosmos it is useless to apply the results of our earthly research. The nature of our present-day education is such that we are prone to apply to the whole cosmos what we consider true in our little earth cell; but it is obvious that truth cannot come to light in this way.

If we proceed from considerations of this sort, a good deal of

38

what confronted men in former times through a primitive, but penetrating, clairvoyant way of looking at things takes on greater value than it has for present-day mankind in general. We will not even pass by the knowledge that came into being in the pastoral life of primitive times, which is nowadays so superficially ignored; for those old shepherds dreamt many a solution to the mysteries of the stars better than can be computed today by our clever scientists with their observatories and spectroscopes. Strange as that may sound, it is true. By studying in a spiritual-scientific way what has been preserved from olden times we can find our way into this mysterious connection we have with the cosmos. Let me tell you here of what can be discovered if we seek through spiritual science the deeply religious and ethical, but also social import of the old *Druidic Mysteries* on the one hand, and those of the *Mithras Mysteries* on the other; for this will give us points of contact with the way in which we should conceive the shaping of a Michael Festival.

Regarding the Druid Mysteries, the lecture cycle I gave a few weeks ago in Penmaenmawr,* Wales—the spot in England that lies exactly behind the island of Anglesea—is of quite special significance because in that place many reminders of the old sacrificial sanctuaries and Mystery temples of the Druids are to be found lying about in fragments. Today these relics, these cromlechs and mounds, are not really very impressive. One climbs up to the mountain tops and finds stones arranged in such a way as to form a sort of chamber, with a larger stone on top; or one sees the cromlechs arranged in circles—originally there were always twelve. In the immediate vicinity of Penmaenmawr were to be found two such sun-circles adjoining each other; and in this particular neighborhood, where even in the spiritual life of nature there is so much that has a different effect from that of nature elsewhere, what I have set forth in various anthroposoph-

---

*See: Rudolf Steiner, *Evolution of the World and Humanity,* Anthroposophic Press, New York.

ical lectures concerning the Druid Mysteries could be tested with the utmost clarity. There is indeed a quite special spiritual atmosphere in this region where—on the island of Anglesea— the Society of King Arthur had a settlement. I must describe it as follows:

In speaking of supersensible things we cannot form thoughts in the same way as we usually do in life or in science, where abstract thoughts are formed, conclusions drawn, and so forth. But to be reduced, in addition, even to speaking more or less abstractly—our language, which has become abstract, demands this—well, if we want to describe something in a spiritual-scientific way we cannot be as abstract as all that in the inner being of our soul: everything must be presented pictorially. We must have pictures, imaginations, before the mind's eye. And this means something different from having thoughts. Thoughts in the soul are extraordinarily patient, according to the degree of our inner indolence: we can hold them; but imaginations always lead a life of their own: we feel quite clearly that an imagination presents itself to us. It is different from writing or drawing, yet similar. We write or draw with our soul; but imaginations are not abstractly held fast like mere thoughts: we *write* them. In most parts of Europe where civilization has already taken on so abstract a character these imaginations flit past comparatively very quickly: depicting the supersensible always involves an inner effort. It is as though we wrote something that would then be immediately wiped away by some demonic power—gone again at once. The same is true of imaginations by means of which we bring the supersensible to consciousness and experience it in our soul.

Now, the spiritual atmosphere in the region of Wales that I mentioned has this peculiarity: while imaginations stamp themselves less readily into the astral element, they persist longer, being more deeply imprinted. That is what appears so conspicuous in that locality; and indeed, everything there points to a more

40

spiritual way of retracing the path to what those old Druid priests really strove for—not during the decadence of the Druid cults, when they contained much that was rather distasteful and even nefarious, but in the time of their flowering.

Examining one of these cromlechs we find it to close off, in a primitive way, a certain space for a chamber that was covered for reasons having to do with the priest's purposes. When you observe sunlight you have first the physical sunlight. But this physical sunlight is wholly permeated by the spiritual activities of the sun; and to speak of the physical sunlight merely as does the modern physicist would be exactly the same as talking about a man's muscles, bones, blood, and so on, omitting all reference to the soul and spirit holding sway within him. Light is by no means mere *phos:* it is *phosphoros,* light-bearing—is endowed with something active and psychic. But this psychic element of light is lost to man in the mere sense-world.—Now, when the Druid priest entered this burying place—like other old cult sanctuaries, the cromlechs were mostly erected over graves—he set up this arrangement which in a certain way was impervious to the physical sun-rays; but the spiritual activities of the sun penetrated it, and the Druid priests were specially trained to perceive these. So he looked through these stones—they were always specially selected—into the chamber where the spiritual activity of the sun penetrated, but from which the physical effect was excluded. His vision had been finely schooled, for what can be seen in a primitive darkroom of that sort varies according to the date, whether February, July, August, or December. In July it is lightly tinged with yellow; in December it radiates a faintly bluish shade from within. And one capable of observing this beholds—in the qualitative changes undergone in the course of the year by this shadow-phenomenon enclosed in such a darkroom—the whole cycle of the seasons in the psycho-spiritual activity of the sun's radiance.

And further: these sun-circles are arranged in the number

twelve, like the twelve signs of the zodiac; and on the mountain we had climbed we found a large sun-circle and nearby a smaller one. If one had ascended, perhaps in a balloon, and looked down upon these two Druid circles, ignoring the insignificant distance between them, the same ground plan would have presented itself—there is something profoundly moving about this—as that of the Goetheanum in Dornach which was destroyed by fire.

The old Druid priests had schooled themselves to read from what thus met their soul's eye how, at every time of day and at every season of the year as well, the sun's shadow varied. They could trace these shadow formations and by means of them determine accurately, This is the time of March, this is the time of October. Through the perception this brought them they were conscious of cosmic events, but also of cosmic conditions having significance for life on this earth. And now, think how people go about it today when they want to determine the influence of cosmic life on earthly life—even the peasants! They have a calendar telling what should be done on this or that day, and they do it, too, approximately; for the fundamental knowledge once available concerning these matters has vanished. But calendars there were none at the time of the old Druids, nor even writing: what the Druid priest was able to tell from his observations of the sun constituted men's knowledge of the connection between the heavens and the earth. And when the priest said: The position of the sun now calls for the sowing of wheat, or, it is the time to lead the bull through the herd, it was done. The cult of that epoch was anything but an abstract prayer: it regulated life in its obvious, practical demands in accord with the enlightenment obtained by communicating with the spirit of the universe. The great language of the heavens was deciphered, and then applied to earthly things.

All this penetrated even the most intimate details of the social life. The priest indicated, according to his readings in the universe, what should be done on such and such a day of the year in order to achieve a favorable contact with the whole universe. That was a cult that actually made of the whole of life a sort of divine worship. By comparison, the most mystical mysticism of our time is a kind of abstraction, for it lets outer nature go its way, so to speak, without bothering about it; it lives and has its being in tradition and seeks inner exaltation, shutting itself off and concentrating within itself as far as possible in order to arrive at an abstract connection with some chimerical world of divine spirit. All this was very different in those olden times. Within the cult—and it was a cult that had a real, true connection with the universe—men united with what the Gods were perpetually creating and bringing about in the world; and as earth-men they carried out the will of the Gods as read in the stellar script by means of the methods known to the Druid priests. But they had to know how to read the writing in the stars.—It is profoundly affecting to be able, at the very spot, to transport oneself back to conditions such as I have described as prevailing during the height of the Druid culture. Elsewhere in that region as well—even over as far as Norway—are to be found many such relics of the Druid culture.

Similarly, all through Central Europe, in parts of Germany, in the Rineland, even in western France, relics and reminders of the ancient *Mithras Cult* are to be found. Here again I will only indicate the most important features. The outer symbol of the Mithras Cult is always a bull ridden by a man thrusting a sword into the bull's neck; below, a scorpion biting the bull, or, a serpent; but whenever the representation is complete you will see this picture of bull and man surrounded by the firmament, and particularly by the signs of the zodiac. Again we ask, What does this picture express? The answer will never be found by an external, antiquated science of history, because the latter has no means of establishing the interrelationships that can provide clues to the meaning of this man on the bull. In order to arrive at the solution one must know the nature of the training undergone by those who served the Mithras Cult. The whole ceremony could, of course, be run off in such a way as to be beautiful—or ugly, if you like—without anything intelligent transpiring. Only one who had passed through a certain training could make sense of it. That is why all the descriptions of the Mithras Mysteries are really twaddle, although the pictures give promise of yielding so much. The service of the Mithras Cult demanded in the neophyte a very fine and sensitive development of the capacity for receptive sentience. Everything depended upon the development of this faculty in him.

I said yesterday in the public lecture * that the human heart is really a subconscious sense organ: subconsciously the head perceives through the heart what goes on in the physical functions of the lower body and the chest. Just as we perceive outer events in the sense-world through the eye, so the human heart is in reality a sense organ in its relation to the functions mentioned. Subconsciously by means of the heart the head, and particularly the cerebellum, perceives the blood being nourished by the transformed foodstuffs, perceives the functioning of the kidneys, the liver, and other processes of the organism. The heart is the sense organ for perceiving all this in the upper portion of the human being.

Now, to raise this heart as a sense organ to a certain degree of consciousness was the object in the schooling of those who were to be engaged in the Mithras Cult. They had to develop a sensitive, conscious feeling for the processes in the liver, kidneys, spleen, etc., in the human organism. The upper man, the head-man, had to sense very delicately what went on in the chest-man and the limb-man. In older epochs that sort of schooling was not the mental training to which we are accustomed today, but a schooling of the whole human being, appealing in the main to the capacity for feeling. And just as we say, on the basis of

*See footnote, page 33.

outer optical perception, There are rain clouds, or, the sky is blue, so the sufficiently matured disciple could say, Now the metabolism in my organism is of this nature, now it is of that. Actually, the processes within the human organism seem the same the year round only to the abstractionist. When science will once more have advanced to real truths concerning these things, men will be amazed to learn how they can establish, by means very different from the crude methods of our modern precision instruments, how the condition of our blood varies and the digestion functions differently in January from September, and in what way the heart as a sense organ is a marvellous barometer for the course of the seasons within the human limb-metabolic organism. The Mithras disciple was taught to perceive the course of the seasons within himself by means of his heart organization, his heart-science, which transmitted to him the passage of food transformed by digestion and taken into the blood. And what was there perceived really showed in man—in the motion of the inner man—the whole course of outer nature.

Oh, what does our abstract science amount to, no matter how accurately we describe plants and plant cells, animals and animal tissue, compared with what once was present instinctively by reason of man's ability to make his entire being into an organ of perception, to develop his capacity for feeling into an organ capable of gleaning knowledge! Man bears within him the animal nature, and truly he does so more intensively than is usually imagined; and what the ancient Mithras followers perceived by means of their heart-science could not be represented otherwise than by the bull. The forces working through the metabolic-limb man, and tamed only by the upper man, are indicated by all that figures as the scorpion and the serpent winding around the bull. And the human being proper, in all his frailty, is mounted above in his primitive might, thrusting the sword of Michael into the neck of the bull. But what it was that must thus be conquered, and how it manifests itself in the course of the seasons, was known only to those who had been schooled in these matters.

Here the symbol begins to take on significance. By means of ordinary human knowledge no amount of observation or picturesque presentation will make anything of it. It can only be understood if one knows something about the heart-science of the old Mithras pupils; for what they really studied when they looked at themselves through their heart was the spirit of the sun's annual passage through the zodiac. In this way the human being experienced himself as a higher being, *riding* on his lower nature; and therefore it was fitting that the cosmos should be arranged in a circle around him: in this manner cosmic spirituality was experienced.

The more a renascent spiritual science makes it possible for us to examine what was brought to light by an ancient semiconscious, dreamlike clairvoyance—but clairvoyance, nevertheless—the greater becomes our respect for it. A spirit of reverence for the ancient cultures pervades us when we see deeper into them and rediscover, for example, that the purpose of the Mithras Cult was to enable the priest, by penetrating the secrets of the seasons' cycle, to tell the members of his community what should be done on each day of the year. The Mithras Cult served to elicit from the heavens the knowledge of what should take place on earth. How infinitely greater is the enthusiasm, the incentive, for what must be done on earth if a man feels himself to be active in such a way that into his activity there flow the impulses deciphered from the great cosmic script he had read in the universe; that he made such knowledge his starting point and employed the resulting impulses in the ordinary affairs of daily life! However little this may accord with our modern concepts—naturally it does not—it was good and right according to the old ones. But in making this reservation we must clearly understand what it means to read in the universe what should be done in the lives of men on earth, thereby knowing ourself to be one with the divine in us—as over against debating the needs of the social life in the vein of Adam Smith or Karl Marx. Only one who can visualize this contrast is able to see clearly into the nature of the new impulses demanded by the social life of our time.

This foundation alone can induce the right frame of mind for letting our cognition pass from the earth out into cosmic space: instead of abstractly calculating and computing and using a spectroscope, which is the common method when looking up to Mercury, Venus, Saturn, and so on, we thereby employ the means comprised in imagination, inspiration, and intuition. In that way, even when only imagination enters in, the heavenly bodies become something very different from the picture they present to modern astronomy—a picture derived partly from sense observation, partly from deductions. The moon, for example, appears to present-day astronomers as some sort of a superannuated heavenly body of mineral which, like a kind of mirror, reflects the sunlight that then, under certain conditions, falls on the earth. They do not bother very much about any of the effects of this sunlight. For a time these observations were applied to the weather, but the excessively clever people of the 19th Century naturally refused to believe in any relation between the various phases of the moon and the weather. Yet those who, like Gustav Theodor Fechner, harbored something of a mystic tendency in their soul, did believe in it. I have repeatedly told the story in our circles about the great 19th Century botanist Schleiden and Gustav Theodor Fechner, both active at the same university. Schleiden naturally considered it a mere superstition that Fechner should keep careful statistics on the rainfall during the full moon and the new moon periods. What Fechner had to say about the moon's influence on the weather amounted to pure superstition for Schleiden. But then the following episode occurred. The two professors had wives; and in those days it was still customary in Leipsic to collect rainwater for the laundry.

Barrels were set up for this purpose; and Frau Professor Fechner and likewise Frau Professor Schleiden caught rainwater in such barrels, like everybody else. Now, the natural thing would have been for Frau Professor Schleiden to say, It is stupid to bother about what sort of an influence the moon phases have on the rainfall. But although Herr Professor Schleiden considered it stupid to take the matter seriously, Frau Professor Schleiden got into a violent dispute with Frau Professor Fechner because both ladies wanted to set up their barrels in the same place at the same time.—The women knew all about rain from practical experience, though the men on their professorial platforms took quite a different standpoint in the matter.

The external aspects of the moon are as I have described them; but especially after rising from imagination to inspiration are we confronted with its spiritual content. This content of the moon is not just something to be understood in an abstract sense: it is a real moon population; and looked at in a spiritual-scientific way the moon presents itself as a sort of fortress in the cosmos. From the outside, not only the light-rays of the sun but all the external effects of the universe are reflected by the moon down to the earth; but in the interior of the moon there is a complete world that nowadays can be reached only by ascending, in a certain sense, to the spirit world. In older writings on the relation of the moon to other cosmic beings you can find many a hint of this, and compare it with what can now be said by anthroposophy about the nature of the moon.

We have often heard that in olden times men had not only that instinctive wisdom of which I have spoken: they had beings as teachers who never descended into physical bodies—higher beings who occupied etheric bodies only, and whose instruction was imparted to men not by speaking, as we speak today, but by transmitting the wisdom in an inner way, as though inoculating the etheric body with it. People knew of the existence of these higher beings, just as we know that some physical teacher is present; but they also knew that these beings surrounded them in a strictly spiritual state. Everything connected with that "primordial wisdom", recognized even by the Catholic Church— the primordial wisdom that once was available, and of which even the Vedas and the sublime Vedanta philosophy are but faint reverberations—all this can be traced back to the teaching of these higher spiritual beings. That wisdom, which was never written down, was not thought out by man: it grew in him. We must not think of the influence exerted by those primordial teachers as any sort of demonstrating instruction. Just as to-day we learn to speak when we are children by imitating the older people, without any particular instruction—as indeed we develop a great deal as though through inner growth—so the primordial teachers exerted a mysterious influence on people of that ancient time, without any abstract instruction; with the result that at a certain age a man simply knew himself to be knowledgeable. Just as today a child gets his second teeth or reaches puberty at a certain age, so men of old became enlightened in the same way. —Doubtless many a modern college student would be delighted if this sort of thing still happened—if the light of wisdom simply flared up in him without his having to exert himself particularly!

What a very different wisdom that was from anything we have today! It was an organic force in man, related to growth, and other forces. It was simply wisdom of an entirely different nature, and what took place in connection with it I can best explain by a comparison. Suppose I pour some sort of liquid into a glass and then add salt. When the salt is dissolved it leaves the liquid cloudy. Then I add an ingredient that will precipitate the salt, leaving the liquid purer, clearer, while the sediment is denser. Very well: if I want to describe what permeated men during the period of the primordial wisdom, I must say it is a mixture of what is spiritually wholly pure and of a physical animalistic element. When nowadays we think, we imagine our abstract thoughts simply as functioning and holding sway without having any being in us; or again, breathing and the circulation seem like something by themselves, apart. But for primeval man in earlier earth epochs, that was all one: it was simply a case of his having to breathe and of his blood circulating in him; and it was in his circulation that he willed.—Then came the time when human thinking moved higher up toward the head and became purer, like the liquid in the glass, while the sediment, as we may call it, formed below.

This occurred when the primordial teachers withdrew more and more from the earth, when this primal wisdom was no longer imparted in the old way. And whither did these primordial teachers withdraw? We find them again in the moon fortress I spoke of. That is where they are and where they continue to have their being. And what remained on earth was the sediment—meaning the present nature of the forces of propagation. These forces did not exist in their present form at the time when primordial wisdom held sway on earth: they gradually became that way—a sort of sediment. I am not implying that they are anything reprehensible, merely that in this connection they are the sediment. And our present abstract wisdom is what corresponds up above to the solvent liquid. This shows us that the development of humanity has brought about on the one hand the more spiritual features in the abstract sense, and on the other, the coarser animalistic qualities as a sediment.—Reflections of this sort will gradually evoke a conception of the spiritual content of the moon; but it must be remembered that this kind of science, which formerly was rather of a prophetic nature, was inherent in men's instinctive clairvoyance.

Just as we can speak about the moon in this way—that is, about what I may call its population, its spiritual aspect—so we can adopt the same course in the case of Saturn. When, by spiritual-scientific effort, we learn to know Saturn—a little is disclosed through imagination, but far more through inspiration and intuition—we delve ever deeper into the universe, and we

50

find that we are tracing the process of sense perception. We experience this physical process; we see something, and then feel the *red* of it. That is something very different from withdrawing from the physical body, according to the methods you will find described in my books, and then being able to observe the effects of an outer object on the human physical organism; to observe how the ether forces, rising from within, seize on the physico-chemical process that takes place, for example, in the eye during optical perception. In reality, the act of exposing ourself in the ordinary way to the world in perception, even in scientific observation, does not affect us very deeply. But when a man steps out of himself in this way and confronts *himself* in the etheric body and possibly in the astral as well, and then sees *ex postfacto* how such a sense-process of perception or cognition came about—even though his spiritual nature had left his physical sense-nature—then he indeed feels a mighty, intensive process taking place in his spirituality. What he then experiences is real ecstasy. The world becomes immense; and what he is accustomed to seeing only in his outer circle of vision, namely, the zodiac and its external display of constellations, becomes something that arises from within him. If someone were to object that what thus arises might be mere recollections, this would only prove that he does not know the event in question; for what arises there are truly not recollections but mighty imaginations transfused by intuitions: here we begin to behold from within what we had previously seen only from without. As human beings we become interwoven with all the mysteries of the zodiac; and if we seize the favorable moment there may flash before us, out of the inner universe, the secret of Saturn, for example, in its passage across the zodiac. Reading in the cosmos, you see, consists in finding the methods for reading out of the inwardly seen heavenly bodies as they pass through the zodiac. What the individual planet tells us provides the vowels of the world-script; and all that forms around the vowels when the planets pass the

51

zodiacal constellations gives us the consonants, if I may use this comparison. By obtaining an inner view of what we ordinarily observe only from the outside we really learn to know the essence of what pertains to the planets.

That is the way to become acquainted with Saturn, for example, in its true inner being. We see its population, which is the guardian of our planetary system's memory: everything that has ever occurred in our planetary system since the beginning of time is preserved by the spirits of Saturn as in a mighty cosmic memory. So if anyone wants to study the great cosmic-historical course of our planetary system, surely he should not speculate about it, as did Kant and Laplace who concluded that once there was a primordial mist that condensed and got into a spiral motion from which the planets split off and circled around the sun, which remained in the middle. I have spoken of this repeatedly and remarked how nice it is to perform this experiment for the children: you have a drop of oil floating on some liquid; above the liquid you have a piece of cardboard through which you stick a pin, and you now rotate the drop of oil by twirling the pin, with the result that smaller drops of oil split off. Now, it may be a good thing in life to forget oneself; but in a case like this we should not forget what we ourselves are doing in the experiment, namely, setting the drop of oil in motion. And by the same token, we should not forget the twirler in the Kant-Laplace theory: we would have to station him out in the universe and think of him as some great and mighty school teacher twirling the pin. Then the picture would have been true and honest; but modern science is simply not honest when dealing with such things.

I am describing to you how one really arrives at seeing what lives in the planets and in the heavenly bodies in general. By means of Saturn we must study the constitution of the planetary system in its cosmic-historical evolution. Only a science that is spiritual can offer the human soul anything that can seem like a cosmic experience. Nowadays we really think only of earthly experiences. Cosmic experience leads us out to participation in the cosmos; and only by co-experiencing the cosmos in this way will we once more achieve a spiritualized instinct for the meaning of the seasons with which our organic life as well as our social life is interwoven—an instinct for the very different relation in which the earth stands to the cosmos while on its way from spring to summer, and again from summer through autumn into winter. We will learn to sense how differently life on earth flows along in the burgeoning spring than when the autumn brings the death of nature; we will feel the contrast between the awakening of life in nature during spring and its sleeping state in the fall. In this way man will again be able to conform with the course of nature, celebrating festivals that have social significance, in the same way that the forces of nature, through his physical organization, make him one with his breathing and his circulation. If we consider what is inside our skin we find that we live there in our breathing and in our circulation. What we are there we are as physical men; in respect of what goes on in us we belong to cosmic life. Outwardly we live as closely interwoven with outer nature as we do inwardly with our breathing and circulation.

And what is man really in respect of his consciousness? Well, he is really an earthworm—and worse: an earthworn for whom it never rains! In certain localities where there is a great deal of rain, it is so pleasant to see the worms coming out of the ground—we must be careful not to tread on them, as will everyone be who loves animals. And then we reflect: Those poor little chaps are down there underground all the time and only come out when it rains; but if it does not rain, they have to stay below. Now, the materialist of today is just such an earthworm—but one for whom it never rains; for if we continue with the simile, the rain would consist of the radiant shining into him of spiritual enlightenment, otherwise he would always be crawling about down there where there is no light. Today humanity must overcome this earthworm nature: it must emerge, must get into the light, into the spiritual light of day. And the call for a Michael Festival is the call for the spiritual light of day.

That is what I wanted to point out to you before I can speak of the things that can inaugurate a Michael Festival as a festival of especial significance—significant socially as well.

IV

THE aim of everything we have been considering during the last three days, my dear friends, has been to point the way in which the human being can once more be converted, as it were, from an earth citizen to a citizen of the cosmos, how the horizon of his life can be expanded to the reaches of the universe, and how thereby his earthly life, too, can be enriched, not only as regards such expansion, but in the intensity of his inner impulses as well.

Yesterday I told you how a genuine spiritual approach can disclose the true nature of the planets: that they are not the mere physical bodies of which modern astronomy tells us, but rather that they can enter our consciousness as manifestations of spiritual beings. In this connection I spoke of the moon and of Saturn. It is not possible in the allotted time to consider each separate planet, nor is it necessary for our present purposes. My aim was merely to point out how our whole frame of mind can be expanded from the earth to cosmic space. But only in this way does it become possible to feel the outer world as part of ourself, in the same way as we do all that takes place inside our skin—our breathing, circulation, and so forth.

Present-day natural science considers our earth merely a dead mineral body. In our civilization it never occurs to a man who is studying some aspect of cosmology, for example, that there is no element of reality in what he has in mind. The present frame of mind is astonishingly obtuse in the matter of a feeling for reality. People cheerfully call a saline crystal "real", and also a rose, without in any way differentiating these realities from each other. Yet a saline crystal is a self-contained reality bounded within itself, while a rose is not. A rose can have no existence other than in connection with the rosebush. A rose—

I refer to the flower—cannot come into being of itself. So if we imagine the flower of a rose at all—even if it fills us with delight to see this conception realized—we have an abstraction, for all that we can touch it: we have not the reality represented by the rosebush. Nor is there any true reality in that earth of primitive rock, slate, limestone, etc., described by modern external science, for there is no such earth as that: it is purely fictitious. Has not the earth produced substantial plants, animals, human beings? That is all part of the earth, just as much as is the crystalline slate of mountain ranges; and if I only consider an earth consisting of stone I have no earth at all. Nothing that external natural science deals with today in any branch of geology is a reality.

So what we should do in this our last lecture is to proceed not only logically but realistically. The obvious errors in the general knowledge of today are not very formidable obstacles because they can readily be refuted. The worst evil in present-day knowledge and cognition is what appears to be absolutely irrefutable. You see, the calculation of everything in the modern science of geology that pertains, for instance, to the origin of the earth, so and so many million years ago, calls for mental brilliance and exact knowledge. True, these calculations disagree by a trifle: some call it twenty million years, others two hundred million; but people of today take such figures in their stride—in other fields as well.* In spite of all this, however, the method employed for such computations really calls for the greatest respect. It is exact, it is accurate—but in what way? It is comparable to the following procedure: I examine a human heart today, and then again in a month. By some sort of more sensitive examination I discover changes in this human heart, so I know how it has altered in the course of a month. Then I

---

*In the matter of post-war inflation, for example, the situation reached a point in 1923 at which 2 billion Marks had the value of 1 pre-war Mark.

observe it again after the lapse of another month, and so forth; that is, I apply the same method to the human heart that geologists use to calculate geologic epochs by millions of years: they compute the little changes by the variations of deposits in the strata, and so forth, in order to arrive at the time lapses. But what am I going to do with the conclusions arrived at concerning the changes in the human heart? I can apply that method to these changes and figure out how this human heart looked three hundred years ago and how it will look in another three hundred years. The calculation may be quite correct, only this heart was not in existence three hundred years ago, nor will it be three hundred years hence.—Similarly, the most brilliant and exact methods of computation tempt the present science of geology into setting forth how the earth looked three million years ago, when there was no trace of Silurian or other strata. Again, the figures can be perfectly correct, but the earth was not in existence. The physicists today calculate the changes that will occur in various substances in twenty million years. In this direction American scientists have done some extraordinarily interesting research and have told us, for instance, how albumen is going to look then—only the earth will no longer be in existence as a physical cosmic body.

Logical methods, then—exactitude—these really constitute the greatest danger, because they are incapable of refutation. Given the correct method, a statement of what the heart looked like three hundred years ago, or how the earth appeared two hundred million years ago, cannot be disproved, nor would it be of any avail to occupy oneself with such refutations: what we need is a realistic way of thinking, a realistic way of looking at the world.

The indispensable factor in every domain of spiritual science is just such a universal grasp of reality; and by means of such methods as I have described—inner, intimate methods that lead to an acquaintance with the population of the moon and that of

Saturn—one learns as well, not only the relation of the earth to its own beings, but the relation of every being of the universe to the being of the cosmos. Everywhere in the world matter contains spirit, for matter is, of course, only the expression of spirit. At every point imagination, inspiration, and intuition find the spirit in the sensible, in the physical—not as enclosed in sharp contours, but as incessant mobility, as perpetual life. And just as there is no reality in the stone formations offered us by geology—for it is a matter of seeking the earth, including its production of plants, animals and physical men—so, if it is to be grasped in its all-embracing entirety, the earth must be understood as the outer, physical configuration of spirit.

Through imagination we learn first how the spirit principle of the earth differs from that of the human being, if I may so express it. In confronting someone, I perceive many different expressions of his being: I notice how he walks, I hear how he speaks, I see his physiognomy and the gestures of his hands and arms; but all this impels me to seek a homogeneous psycho-spiritual principle dominating him. And just as here one instinctively searches for a unified psycho-spiritual principle in the self-enclosed human being, so imaginative cognition, in contemplating the earth, finds not an undivided earth-spirit principle, but a multiplicity of manifold variety. It is therefore wrong to infer by analogy, for example, a homogeneous spirit principle in the earth from the spirit principle of man; for true vision reveals a multiplicity of earth spirituality, of spiritual beings, as it were, that dwell in the kingdoms of nature. But these spiritual beings are passing through a life: they are in a process of becoming.

Now let us see what this imagination perceives during the course of a year in the way of earth activity when it is supplemented by inspiration, and we will direct our soul's gaze first to the winter. Outwardly, frost and snow cover the ground, and the germs of the earth beings, of the plants, so to speak, are received back into the earth. All that is connected with the earth as germination—we can here ignore the world of animals and men—is withdrawn by the earth into itself. In addition to the familiar burgeoning life of spring and summer, winter shows us dying life. But what does this dying life of winter mean in a spiritual sense? It means that those spiritual beings whom we call elemental spiritual beings—beings that constitute the life-giving principle proper, especially in plants—withdraw into the earth itself and become intimately connected with it. Such is the imaginative aspect of the earth in winter: it takes into its body, as it were, its spiritual elemental beings and shelters them there. In winter the earth is at its most spiritual; that is, it is most fully permeated by its elemental spirit-beings.

Like all supersensible observation, all this passes over into feeling, into sensibility, in him who envisions it. As he feelingly observes the earth in winter and sees the snow on the ground, he knows that this makes a covering for the earth's body so that within it the elemental spirit-beings of earth life themselves may dwell. With the coming of spring the relation of these beings to the earth is transformed into a relation to the cosmic environment. Everything in these beings that during the winter had produced a close relationship with the earth itself becomes related to the cosmic environment in spring: the elemental beings seek to escape out of the earth; and spring really consists of the earth's sacrificial devotion to the universe in letting its elemental beings flow out into it. In winter these elemental beings need repose in the bosom of the earth; in spring they need to stream up through the air, through the atmosphere —to be determined by the spiritual forces of the planetary system, namely, of Mercury, Mars, Jupiter, and so on. Nothing that can act upon the earth spirits from the planetary system does so in winter: this commences in the spring. And here we can observe a more spiritual cosmic process, and compare it with a corresponding but more material one in the human being: our breathing process. We inhale the outer air, hold it in our own body, then exhale it again. In-breathing, out-breathing—that is one component of human life.

Now, in the winter the earth has inhaled its whole spirituality, and with the commencement of spring it starts to exhale it again into the cosmos. In the very old periods of human evolution, when there still existed a sort of instinctive clairvoyance, men felt this; and therefore they felt it to be in conformity with earth existence to celebrate the Christmas Festival during the winter solstice. Then the earth was at its most spiritual—that was the time when it could hold the mystery of the Christmas Festival. The Redeemer could unite only with an earth that had drawn all its spirituality into itself. But for the festival intended to induce a feeling in man that he belongs not only to the earth but to the whole universe, that as an earth citizen his soul can be awakened through cosmic agencies, for this festival of resurrection only that season could serve which carries all the spirituality of the earth out into the cosmos. That is why we find the Christmas Festival linked with phenomena pertaining to the earth, with the dark of winter, with a sort of earth sleep, while on the other hand we see the Easter Festival so fitted into the course of the seasons that we determine it not by earthly but by cosmic events: the first Sunday after the first full moon of spring. It was the stars that in former times had to tell men when Easter should be celebrated—the time when the whole earth opens itself to the cosmos. One resorted to the cosmic script: man had to become aware that he is an earth being, and that at the Spring Festival of Easter he has to open himself to cosmic reaches.

It positively hurts to hear people discussing such glorious thoughts of a bygone age as they have been doing now for twenty or twenty-five years: well-meaning people who do not want the Easter Festival to be so movable. At the very least, they say, it should be held on the first Sunday in April; they want it all quite external and abstract. I have had to listen to arguments pointing out that it creates confusion in commercial ledgers to have Easter so movable, and that business could be carried on in a much more regular way if the date of Easter were strictly assigned. It is really distressing to see how world-alien our civilization has become—this civilization that fancies itself practical. A suggestion such as the one just mentioned is as unpractical as can be, because our civilization can establish something that may be practical for a day, but never for a century. In order to be practical for a century, the matter in question must be in harmony with the universe. But herein the cycle of the seasons must ever be able to point man to his inner life in conjunction with the entire cosmos.

Advancing from spring toward summer, the earth more and more loses its inner spirituality. This spirituality, these elemental beings, pass from the terrestrial to the extra-terrestrial realm and come wholly under the influence of the cosmic, planetary world; and in a former epoch this was celebrated in the great and profound rites performed in certain Mysteries at the height of summer, the season in which we have instituted the Festival of St. John. This was the time when the initiates of yore, the Mystery priests of those sanctuaries where the St. John Festival was celebrated in its original significance, were deeply permeated with the contemplation: That which in the winter time, during the winter solstice, I had to seek by gazing into the interior of the earth through the blanket of snow that became transparent for me, that I will now find by directing my vision outward; and the elemental beings that during the winter were determined by what pertains to the inner earth, these are now determined by the planets. From the beings which in winter I had to seek in the earth I gather, at the height of summer, knowledge of their experiences with the planets.—And just as we experience our respiratory process unconsciously, simply as something inwardly a part of our existence, so man once experienced his existence as a part of the course of the seasons in the spirituality that pertains to the earth. In winter he sought his kindred elemental nature-beings in the depths of the earth, in midsummer he sought them high in the clouds. In the earth he found them inwardly permeated and saturated with their own earth forces coupled with what the moon forces have left behind in the earth; and in the summertime he found them given over to the vast universe.

And when summer begins to wane after the St. John season, the earth starts inbreathing its spirituality again; and once more the time approaches for the earth to harbor its spirituality within.

We are nowadays little inclined to observe this in- and out-breathing of the earth. Human respiration is more a physical process; the breathing of the earth is a spiritual process—the passing out of the elemental earth-beings into cosmic space and their reimmersion in the earth. Yet it is a fact that just as we participate, in the tenor of our inner life, in what goes on in our circulation, so, as true human beings, we take part in the cycle of the seasons. As the blood circulation inside us is essential for our existence, the circulation of the elemental beings between earth and the heavens is indispensable for us as well; and only the bluntness of their sensibility prevents men today from glimpsing the factors within themselves that are conditioned by this external course of the year.* But the very necessity which in the course of time will compel men to learn to receive the ideas of spiritual science, of supersensible cognition—the necessity to develop the inner activity indispensable for a full realization of what spiritual-scientific revelations entrust them with—this in itself will sharpen and refine their capacity for sentient receptivity.

This, my dear Friends, is what you really should await as a result of deep absorption in that supersensible cognition aimed at by anthroposophy. You see, if you read a book or a lecture

---

See: Rudolf Steiner, *Calendar of the Soul,* Anthroposophic Press, New York.

cycle on anthroposophy just as you read any other book—that is, as abstractly as you read other books—there is no point whatever in reading anthroposophic literature at all. In that case I should advise reading cookery books or technical books on mechanics: that would be more useful; or read about *How to Become a Good Business Man*. Reading books or listening to lectures on anthroposophy has sense only when you realize that to receive its messages a frame of mind is called for totally different from the one involved in the gleaning of other information. This is confirmed even by the fact that those who today fancy themselves particularly clever consider anthroposophic literature quite mad. Well, they must have a reason for this view, and it is this: Everybody else describes things quite differently, presents the world in an entirely different way; and we cannot stand these anthroposophists who come along and change it all around.

And indeed, the conclusions reached by anthroposophy and appearing in the world today are very different from what emanates from other quarters; and I must say that a certain policy adhered to by some of our friends, namely, that of making anthroposophy generally palatable by minimizing the discrepancies between it and the trivial opinions of others—such efforts cannot be approved at all, though they are frequently met with. What is needed is a totally different attitude, a different orientation of the soul, if the message of anthroposophy is to be considered plausible, comprehensible, understandable, intelligent—instead of mad.

But given this different orientation, not only the human intellect but the human *Gemüt* will in a short time undergo a schooling that will render it more sensitive to impressions: it will no longer feel winter merely as the time for donning a heavy coat, or summer as the signal for shedding various articles of clothing; but rather, it will learn to feel the subtle transitions occurring in the course of the year, from the cold snow of winter to the sultry midsummer of earth life. We shall learn to sense the course of the year as we do the expressions of a living, soul-endowed being. Indeed, the proper study of anthroposophy can bring us to the point at which we feel the manifestations of the seasons as we do the assent or dissent in the soul of a friend. Just as in the words of a friend and in the whole attitude of his soul we can perceive the warm heartbeat of a soul-endowed being whose manner of speaking to us is quite different from that of a lifeless thing, so nature, hitherto mute, will begin to speak to us as though out of her soul. In the cycle of the seasons we shall learn to feel soul, soul in the process of becoming; we will learn to listen to what the year as the great living being has to tell us, instead of occupying ourself only with little living beings; and we shall find our place in the whole soul-endowed cosmos.

But then, when summer passes into autumn, and winter approaches, something very special will speak to us out of nature. One who has gradually acquired the sensitive feeling for nature just described—and anthroposophists will notice in due time that this can indeed be brought about in the soul, in the *Gemüt,* through anthroposophical endeavor—such a one will learn to distinguish between nature-consciousness, engendered during the spring and summer, and self-consciousness proper which thrives in the fall and winter. What is nature-consciousness? When spring comes, the earth develops its sprouting, blossoming life; and if I react to this in the right way, if I let all that the spring really embraces speak within me—I need not be conscious of it: it speaks to the unconscious depths of a consummate human life as well—if I achieve all this I do not merely say, The flower is blooming, the plant is germinating, but I feel a true concord with nature and can say, My ego blooms in the flower, my ego germinates in the plant. Nature-consciousness is engendered only by learning to take part in all that develops in the burgeoning and unfolding life of nature. To be able to germinate with the plant, to blossom with the plant, to bear fruit with the plant, that is what is meant by "passing out of one's own inner self" and by "becoming one with outer nature". Truly, the term "to develop spirituality" does not mean to become abstract: it means to be able to follow the spirit in its being and expansion. And if, by participating in the germinating, the flowering, and the bearing fruit, man develops this delicate feeling for nature during the spring and summertime, he prepares himself to live in devotion to the universe, to the firmament, precisely at the height of summer. Every little firefly will be for him a mysterious revelation of the cosmos; every breath in the atmosphere in midsummer will proclaim the cosmic principle within the terrestrial.

But then—if we have learned to feel with nature, to blossom with the flowers, to germinate with the seeds, to take part in the bearing of fruit—then, because we have learned to dwell in nature with our own being, we cannot help co-experiencing the essence of the fall and winter as well. He who has learned to live with nature in the spring learns also to die with nature in the autumn. Thus we attain again by a different way to those sensations that once so intensely permeated the soul of the Mithras priest, as I have described. He sensed the course of the seasons in his own body. That is no longer possible for present-day mankind; but what will become more and more incumbent upon humanity in the near future—and herein anthroposophists must be the pioneers—is to experience the cycle of the seasons: to learn to live with the spring and to die with the autumn.

But man must not die: he must not let himself be overpowered. He can live united with burgeoning, blossoming nature, and in doing so he can develop his nature-consciousness; but when he experiences the dying in nature the experience is a challenge to oppose this dying with the creative forces of his own inner being. Then the spirit-soul principle, his true self-consciousness, will come to life within him; and by sharing in nature's dying during the fall and winter he will become in the highest degree the awakener of his own self-consciousness. In

65

this way the human being evolves: he transforms himself in the course of the seasons by experiencing this alternation of nature-consciousness and self-consciousness. When he takes part in nature's dying, that is the time when his inner life force must awake: when nature draws her elemental beings into herself the inner human force must become the awakening of self-consciousness.

Michael forces! Now we feel them again. In the old days of instinctive clairvoyance the picture of Michael's Combat with the Dragon arose from quite different premises. Now, however, if we vividly comprehend the idea embraced in *nature-consciousness—self-consciousness: spring-summer—autumn-winter,* the end of September will once more reveal to us the same force that points us to the victorious power which should evolve on this grave if we take part in the dying of nature: the victorious power that fans the true, strong self-consciousness of man into bright flame. Here we have again Michael vanquishing the Dragon.

It is indispensable that anthroposophical knowledge, anthroposophical cognition, should stream into the human *Gemüt* as a force. And the way leads from the dry and abstract, although exact conceptions of today to that goal where the living enlightenment taken into our *Gemüt* once more confronts us with something as full of life as was in olden times the glorious picture of Michael in battle with the Dragon. This infuses into our cosmogony something very different from abstract concepts; and furthermore, do not imagine that such experience is without consequences for the totality of man's life on earth!

I have frequently set forth in our meetings here in Vienna how we can enter and feel at home in the consciousness of immortality, in the awareness of prenatal existence. At this meeting I wanted particularly to show you how we can gather into our *Gemüt* the spiritual forces from the spiritual world, in the wholly concrete sense. It is truly not enough to talk in a general, pantheistic, or other vague way about spirit underlying all matter. That would be just as abstract as it would to be satisfied with the truism: Man is endowed with spirit. What possible meaning could that have? The term spirit takes on meaning only when it speaks to us in concrete details, when it keeps revealing itself to us concretely, when it can bring us comfort, uplift, joy. The pantheistic "spirit" in philosophical speculations means nothing whatever. Only the living spirit, that speaks to us in nature in the same way as the human soul in man speaks to us, can enter the human *Gemüt* in a vitalizing and exalting way. But when this does occur our *Gemüt* will derive powers from the enlightenment transformed in it, precisely those powers that are needed in our social life. *During the last three or four centuries mankind has simply acquired the habit of considering all nature, and human existence as well, in intellectual, abstract conceptions; and now that humanity is confronted with the great problems of social chaos, people try to solve these, too, with the same intellectual means. But never in the world will anything but chimeras be brought forth in this way. A consummate human heart is a prerequisite to the right to an opinion in the social realm; but this no man can possess without finding his relation with the cosmos, and in particular, with the spiritual substance of the cosmos.*

When the human *Gemüt* will have received into itself spirit-consciousness—the spirit-consciousness engendered by the transition from nature-consciousness (spring-summer) to self-consciousness (autumn-winter)—then will dawn the solution, among others, of the social problems of the moment. Not the intellectual substance of such problems as the social question, but the forces they need, depend in a deep sense upon the contingency of a sufficient number of men being able to make such spiritual impulses their own.

All this must be brought to our *Gemüt* if we would consider adding the autumn festival, the Michael Festival, to the three we have: the festivals of Christmas, Easter, and St. John, that have become mere shadows. How wonderful it would be if this Michael Festival could be celebrated at the end of September with the whole power of the human heart! But never must it be celebrated by making certain arrangements that bring about nothing but abstract *Gemüt* sensations: a Michael Festival calls for human beings who feel in their souls in fullest measure everything that can activate spirit-consciousness.

What does Easter represent in the year's festivals? It is a festival of resurrection. It commemorates the Resurrection realized in the Mystery of Golgotha through the descent of Christ, the Sun-Spirit, into a human body. First death, then resurrection: that is the outer aspect of the Mystery of Golgotha. One who understands the Mystery of Golgotha in this sense sees death and resurrection in this way of redemption; and perhaps he will feel in his soul that he must unite in his *Gemüt* with Christ, the victor over death, in order to find resurrection in death. But Christianity does not end with the traditions associated with the Mystery of Golgotha: it must advance. The human *Gemüt* turns inward and deepens more and more as time goes on; and in addition to this festival that brings alive the Death and Resurrection of Christ, man needs that other one which reveals the course of the year as having its counterpart within him, so that he can find in the round of the seasons first of all the resurrection of the soul—in fact, the necessity for achieving this resurrection—in order that the soul may then pass through the portal of death in a worthy way. Easter: death, then resurrection; Michaelmas: resurrection of the soul, then death. This makes of the Michael Festival a reversed Easter Festival. Easter commemorates for us the Resurrection of Christ from death; but in the Michael Festival we must feel with all the intensity of our soul: In order not to sleep in a half-dead state that will dim my self-consciousness between death and a new birth, but rather, to be able to pass through the portal of death in full alertness, I must rouse my soul through my inner forces before I die. First, resurrection of the soul—then death, so that in death that resurrection can be achieved which man celebrates within himself.

I trust these lectures have contributed a little toward bridging the gap between the purely mental enlightenment anthroposophy has to offer, and what this anthroposophy can mean to the human *Gemüt.* That would make me very happy; and I should be able to look back affectionately on all that we have been privileged to discuss in these lectures, which were truly not addressed to your mind but to your *Gemüt,* and through which, in a manner not customary nowadays, I wanted to point out, among other things, the social stimulus so sorely needed by mankind today. Humanity will become attuned to such social impulses only by an inner deepening of the *Gemüt.* That is what fills my soul, now that I must bring these lectures to a close. It was from an inner need of my heart that I delivered them to you, my dear Austrian friends.